12 CONVERSATIONS

BY: Cathy Sikorski, Esq.

How To Talk to Almost Anyone About Long-Term Care
Planning

For John, Rachel, Margot and Mom

My biggest cheerleaders who have never failed to support me or challenge me.

I love you beyond measure.

Published 2021 by Corner Office Books
Printed in the United States of America

ISBN: 978-1-7372746-4-3

Cover art and design by Dwayne Booth

Author photo by Leigh-Ann Kline of L.A. Kline Portrait, LLC

TABLE OF CONTENTS

CHAPTER ONE

A CONVERSTION WITH MYSELF!

This is a book for when people are sick not dead. This is critical because people confuse sick people and dead people. I know, that sounds ridiculous. It's not that you don't know the difference between a sick person and a dead person. It's that we have been so trained to think of preparation in terms of just two things: retirement and death. We forget that there can be a big chasm of illness in the middle and we didn't prepare for that. Even people who take care of their parents seem to forget that this could and is likely to happen to them. That is the whole point of this book. What do I do if I forgot about the missing puzzle piece of what happens between retirement and death? That presumes you make it to retirement without a debilitating illness. Many do not. If they took the advice like the kind you will find here, when an unexpected illness or incapacity came knocking on their door, they and you will have much more peace of mind.

Regardless of your marital status or why you picked up this book, you first need to ask yourself some questions about this aging and caregiving thing. You may be reading to get some quick tips on how to deal with your parents, your in-laws, your aunt, your oldest brother, or your spouse. But you first need to look in the mirror and see how *you feel* about some of these preparation tactics. This is more profound than you might imagine for two reasons:

1. You will have a better understanding of what and how all this legal and financial preparation works.

2. You may very well change your mind about what Mom or Dad *have* to do once you bring in to focus what you want to do for yourself. There are many moving pieces to elder and caregiving preparation. If you will be making those decisions for others, you will be better prepared if you have to do it for yourself first.

How do I talk to myself?

It matters. Hello, You! From this side of the page, I want you to know that you are asking yourself these questions so that you can be as prepared as possible for a crisis. The fact of the matter is: a crisis is a crisis. You can't actually prepare for it completely, but you can be at the ready so that when dealing with the critical decisions, you are able to make them quickly or even slowly if you need time for a decision. Knowing that you have made all the pre-decisions you possibly could to help move along a crisis process will give you peace of mind today and in the future.

Asking yourself serious, hard questions is going to be *de rigeur* here. Pardon my French, but that's the rules. Then, when you are done talking to yourself, you will be ready to do it with all the other people in this book. I will attempt to temper these conversations with those we love and those we work with because this is hard stuff. Having had these conversations so many times, I can't count any more, you will have the benefit of my brilliant moments as well as my dummy moments!

Questions to ask yourself and Two Plans:

Tell me what I want, what I really, really want!

The first thing we need to do is distinguish between what I want when I am alive and what I want when I am dead. Yes, it's that brutal. And it's very, very different. Most people don't realize that you need to make two different plans, the life plan (which they think is the retirement plan, but it isn't) and the death plan, which is well, yeah, the "I won't be back" plan. For both plans you need to ask yourself some meaningful questions.

Plan A (for Alive): The Twin Sisters: Powers of Attorney

Durable Financial Power of Attorney and Heath Care Power of Attorney will be the two most important tools in your toolbox. These are the four questions for Plan A. Let's look at each one and then look in the mirror!

A. If I am incapacitated, who do I want in charge of my finances?

B. If I am incapacitated, who do I want in charge of my health care?

C. If I am incapacitated but still in charge, where do I want to live?

D. If I am not incapacitated, where do I want to live?

Let's first talk about a Durable Financial Power of Attorney:

A. If I am incapacitated, who do I want in charge of my finances?

Yes, you have to put someone else in charge. If you are married and in a good relationship (I do hope that's not a big IF, but if it is, pay attention here) then you will likely choose your spouse to be in charge of your finances.

CAVEAT: JUST BECAUSE YOU HAVE A SPOUSE DOESN'T MEAN THAT HE/SHE IS LEGALLY IN CHARGE OF YOUR FINANCES.

This may be the most devastating news at the worst possible time when a spouse finds out. And it all has to do with the way we save money. This is the most important topic I will cover in this book and I'm putting it right here, right in the beginning in case you get hungry, tired, bored or your dog eats this book. I'm not saving this for the finale. The fireworks are now and you'd better be watching.

Not so long ago, our parents and grandparents saved money with joint savings accounts, defined pensions, joint CD's (not music, certificates of deposit) and joint pretty-much-everything-else. Then came the dawning of the 401K, the IRA, the 403B, the Roth IRA and many such savings plans. These plans were largely supposed to benefit the common person, help her save and basically get employers off the hook for defined pensions. The tricky part is that most of us in the Baby Boomer, Gen X and all the Gens behind us are saving our money in these accounts. Saving our money is great. But you have to know that these 401Ks, IRAs, 403Bs, and Roth IRAs, can only be owned by ONE PERSON. That's right you own it. You and you alone. By legal definition none of these accounts can be joint—ever. If you are married, your spouse does not own your 401K or any of those other things. And if you are incapacitated your spouse has no access to your 401K or anything else you own all by yourself, without the proper paperwork.

My Nana used to go into the bank and tell the teller to give her $20 out of Mike's account. Yes, Mike was my Pop Pop. And yes, the teller did it. I don't even think Nana's name was on that account, but she was Mike's wife and that was good enough for Ethel, the teller. So good, that Nana took eight thousand dollars out of Pop Pop's account and bought them a house on Hanover Street without telling him first.

Please note: those days are over.

Why is this important to you? Well for one thing, if you want someone to handle your affairs because you are temporarily in an induced coma from a car accident, you'd better have that someone in place through the proper paperwork. If the Power of Attorney paperwork is not in order, then you are likely looking at guardianship through the court system. As the one in the coma, you can't tell anyone what to do or how to do it when it comes to your finances. So, who's in charge? How do your bills get paid? Who has access to your money, especially those non-joint accounts like a 401k, IRA, or Roth IRA? If you are *not* the one in a coma, and your spouse *is* the one in the coma, AND that coma-ridden spouse owns those 401k accounts, how do you get to his money?

You need to have access to that sick spouse's money through a Financial Power of Attorney. If you depend on your spouse's retirement funds to live day-to-day, access to those funds though a Power of Attorney is critical. Otherwise, you may have closed that door to access that money for yourself until death do you part. While you are both healthy and competent your need to get this paperwork completed is paramount. And don't sit there all smug telling me you're the beneficiary of your spouse's 401k. Beneficiaries only get money when someone dies. Remember? We are talking about sick people not dead people. Your spouse is sick and you need money. He is not dead in this scenario and you are not a beneficiary, yet. Unless you've decided to go another route and that's a book by a criminal attorney not an Elder Lawyer.

So, what can you do? GET A DURABLE FINANCIAL POWER OF ATTORNEY.

Here's the thirty second definition of a Power of Attorney (POA).

A durable financial power of attorney is a document that you sign, giving the power to your Agent to act as if they are you in all financial transactions and capacity.

Like every lawyer, I'm going to tell you that it looks simple, but it is far more complex than that. Understanding that a POA is a very powerful document and that you need one is the first step in the right direction of planning.

I am also going to tell you that you should consult an attorney, preferably an Elder Lawyer about this very crucial document. This document must meet very strict and very different requirements in each and every state. In some states they are a bit more flexible with language and specifics, giving the benefit of the doubt to the Agent. In other states, not so much. Where I live in Pennsylvania, for example the law is very particular about language in a Power of Attorney especially concerning the transfer of funds for 'gifting' and lest you think that means giving presents to your grandchildren at Christmas, it's much worse than that. "Gifting" can mean the very serious need to transfer large sums of money from a sick spouse's IRA or 401k to a healthy spouse to allow her to continue to live in her home, get her own medical care, or even buy an automobile, which could be denied if the Power of Attorney document doesn't allow 'gifting.'

How is that a *gift* to a *spouse*, you ask? Remember how we save money now? Since only one person can own all those big retirement accounts, to transfer funds *while the owner is living but incapacitated,* is a *gift* to anyone, including a spouse. The spouse has no rights to that money under any other authority. The only way to allow someone into your 401K, IRA, 403B, Roth IRA and likely some other investment tools, is to do so with a durable financial power of attorney because that Agent then has the legal authority to act as if they are the owner of those accounts.

Choose your Agent wisely! They will have an enormous amount of power over your finances. It must be someone you trust to do the right thing. But you must choose.

This is one of the myriad reasons to have a durable financial power of attorney. Know that this document is critical to the care of anyone who has a short-term or long-term incapacitation. That could happen to anyone. I made my 18-year-old college-age children sign both a financial and health care POA before going to college. I did not want a college or hospital administrator telling me they would not share critical information about my child because said child was an "adult." Everyone needs this.

Just as a quick aside, everyone rightly asks, "What does Durable mean here?" A long time ago, when the earth was green, legal scholars decided the word "durable" was necessary if you meant to have a POA last during and/or after an incapacity, so the word, "durable" was critical to note that the POA *endures* even after one is incapacitated or unable to change it in any way. This seems silly since the whole point is to have something *in case you are incapacitated,* but you know lawyers, if it ain't broke, we sure like to fix it.

So, ask yourself these questions:

1. Do I have a Durable Financial Power of Attorney?

2. Who will be my Agent?

   This is a very personal decision. Discuss it with your spouse, if you have one, especially when deciding the alternate agent. If you are single, discuss it with the people you trust to help you with this decision. Also get input from your lawyer and/or financial advisor.

Your Agent will have to work with them so keep that in mind. This person will have the power to act as you in your financial dealings in every possible way. They can get in to your bank accounts, investments, use your credit cards, get a credit card in your name, sell your house, buy a house, sell your car or buy a car all with your money. So, choose wisely. If you find out what happens when you need a POA and you don't have one, that is no laughing matter.

3. Who will be my Alternate Agent?

    Yes, have an alternate because if you and your hubby go on a cruise and you both get into an accident where neither of you can make decisions, who is going to be in charge? Make certain there is an Alternate Agent in your POA, ask your attorney.

4. If I do have a Power of Attorney, is it up-to-date?

    Laws change all the time. People do too. A ten, twenty or thirty-year-old power of attorney document is likely outdated and needs to be redone. Just do it. In Pennsylvania the legislature made sweeping changes in 2015 for Powers of Attorney (like that need for specific gifting language we talked about) and updated some more issues concerning POAs a few years later. Legislators don't know or care if you keep up with what they are doing. Talk to your lawyer if you haven't done these documents recently. Do the same for your parents or anyone else you may be a caregiver for.

5. If I don't have a Power of Attorney, how do I get it?

    If you have an attorney, ask her if they do Elder Law in her firm. If they don't, ask for a referral. All lawyers do not know all law things. You wouldn't go to your primary care physician for a heart transplant. If you don't know or have a lawyer, your local bar association in your county or state surely has a research tool for a local Elder Lawyer. You can also look for a CELA (Certified Elder Lawyer) or someone in NAELA (National Association of Elder Lawyers). I will say there are many qualified attorneys who don't have these designations. There are also many attorneys who do this kind of work and don't keep up with the changes in Elder Law, as well. Elder Law is kind of the new kid in town. It has cropped up and gotten more complicated as we stay alive longer...see not dying...not about dead people. It's a whole area of law for living longer. And it's not been around as an expertise for more than about 30 years or less. So, ask around for referrals, but not just your best friend's cousin who is a lawyer. Make sure this is their jam, so you don't get in a jam!

There are dozens of additional reasons to get a Financial Durable Power of Attorney in place. For example, who will take care of your digital assets, passwords, banking, investments, real estate, credit cards, life insurance, Venmo, Cash App, mortgages, rental payments, car payments, the list is nearly endless. If you don't use Venmo, Cash App, Bitcoin or don't even know what that is then those things aren't on the table for you. However, all the other stuff still applies to you. If you are in charge of someone else's information and assets and they have digital assets then you must talk to them, educate yourself about how these things work and keep that conversation going. Just go and get it done. In Chapter 9, we will review more detailed questions for the conversation with your lawyer. You will know exactly what to ask and what answers should make you comfortable that you have found an attorney who knows how to prepare documents for aging and caregiving inevitabilities.

B. If I am incapacitated, who do I want in charge of my health care?

Health Care Power of Attorney

Much like the Durable Financial Power of Attorney, this important document gives power to your chosen Agent or sometimes called Surrogate to make health care decisions in the case of your incapacitation. Some states also call this a Health Care Proxy.

Practically, the power to make health care decisions by a spouse is usually much more accepted. Very often medical personnel just want to move things forward and whether erroneously or not, they often ask for guidance from a spouse first and ask questions later for legal documentation.

None of this means you shouldn't have a Health Care Power of Attorney. This document is extremely critical in a crisis, especially if the person who is required to make decisions is NOT a spouse. It may be more critical without a crisis, when the health care providers have the time to ask, "Hey, who is in charge here?" If you are caring for someone with a long-term condition, or you have such a condition yourself, now or in your future, you want a Health Care POA in place to hurdle that "Who's the Boss?" conversation as quickly as possible.

There are essentially two parts to a Health Care Power of Attorney:

Health care decisions and End of Life Decisions (also crazy documents called a Living Will or an Advanced Directive)

I. Health Care Decisions:

It's much more complex than you may have imagined. It is not just "Which hospital do we go to?" or "Who's your doctor?" Here are some of the health care concerns a Health Care POA will have to navigate:

- Which hospital *do* we go to? (you gotta'start somewhere)

- Who are the physicians there?

- Do they deal with my loved one's illness?

- Where will my loved one need to go for rehabilitation after hospitalization?

- Who is the insurance carrier?

- What do I have to do to get the insurance carrier to talk to me?

- Who pays for an ambulance?

- Do I get to choose a nursing home?

- Can I choose in-home heath care aides?

- Where do they come from?

- Who pays for that?

- Are there any long-term care insurance benefits?

- Does my loved one have Veteran's benefits?

- Can I talk to the Veteran's benefits people?

- What about the pharmacy?

- Can I pick up prescriptions?

- Can I talk to the pharmacist about concerns of my loved one?

- What about durable medical equipment?

- Who pays for that?

- Where does it come from?

- Will they discuss insurance payments with me from Medicare or Medigap or Medicare Advantage?

- How do I get to speak to all those Medicare people if my loved one is hospitalized and can't communicate?

This is actually a short list of the jobs a Health Care Power of Attorney will be expected to do for you. It's a dubious honor. But clearly you want to choose someone you trust and someone who is going to 'go to bat' for you, especially when you are unwell and need an advocate on your side.

Here are the questions to ask yourself when choosing your Health Care Power of Attorney:

1. Who will be able to make informed medical decisions for me, especially in a crisis?

2. Who is someone who can speak to insurance companies, physicians, hospitals, rehabilitation centers, medical equipment providers, and get results?

3. Who has the understanding of what I truly want done in a medical crisis? Have I communicated that to them?

4. Who can I choose as an alternate in case my first choice is unavailable OR finds they cannot make the hard decisions?

5. If I already have a Health Care Power of Attorney, is it up-to-date and is it still the same Agent I would choose today?

II. End of Life Decisions

Living Wills and Advanced Directives have gotten lots of air time lately, but no one seems to agree on exactly what these documents are, therefore you need to discuss this with your Elder Lawyer to ensure that you have what you need in this area.

Typically, a Living Will is a document that you sign giving someone specific or general authority to decide what to do if you are in a *permanent vegetative state.* That's the most critical piece of a living will. It is to be referred to as a guide when you are permanently unable to decide how you want to live the remainder of your days.

To be blunt: This is a Pull the Plug or Don't Pull the Plug Document.

You need to decide what you would choose *and* who in your life can support that decision. So have a good long, hard talk with yourself about what your choices would be if you were in a permanent vegetative state. I happen to be writing this book during Covid-19 and this is a particularly critical conversation right now. Many Covid patients are experiencing long periods of time where they are in an induced coma in order to heal from this horrific disease. This is not a permanent vegetative state. But it truly begs the question: "What do I want done if I am in such a state?" You need to get this document done and done correctly. You need to be assured that the Living Will and your conversation with your Health Care Agent puts everyone on the same page with your physician at the time to make the decision you truly wish to make.

This does not mean that Covid-19 or any other pandemic is the only reason for a Living Will. These documents have been around for a long time and will continue to be necessary. We live in an age of amazing medical technologies and discoveries. Only you can decide how you want your final days to play out unless you make no advanced decisions and then you leave it up to others, others you may not have chosen to make decisions you may not agree with. Choose. Make a plan that is *your* plan.

Advanced Directives

Advanced Directives are often a misunderstood tool. An Advanced Directive is a document that in some fashion spells out an individual's wishes as to what they would like to see happen in a crisis situation where they are either in that permanent vegetative state OR chronically ill and have made some final decisions in the case of a critical situation. This can cover multiple types of forms including the Living Will we just discussed. It can also include:

- DNR's (Do Not Resuscitate): A medical order written by a physician to not administer CPR or life-saving treatment if the patient has signed this document

- POLST (Physician's Order for Life Sustaining Treatment): In most states this is a hot pink colored document that has directions as to whether the patient requests life-saving treatment or not. It is signed by a physician and is to be kept with the patient at all times.

- FIVE WISHES at fivewishes.org from © 2020 Aging with Dignity or other documents created by many caregiving organizations for discussing and memorializing end-of-life decisions and final health care wishes.

This is a tricky area of Health Care planning. Most of these additional documents are not necessarily used in a permanent vegetative state but they are end-of-life documents in that you are telling *someone* what your wishes are in an end-of-life situation. It's tricky not because you shouldn't tell someone but because you don't know exactly when that situation will arise. Here's a good rule of thumb:

If you are healthy, a Health Care Power of Attorney and a Living Will should cover the bases, *especially*, if you've had a conversation with your Agent (s). This is where talking to others is important, not just to yourself.

If you or your loved one who you are a caregiver for, has real health issues that can imminently lead to prolonged hospitalization, nursing home care, or intensive in-home care, then you need to discuss matters surrounding extraordinary measures of care and decide upon the necessary documents to put in place, such as a DNR, POLST, or disease-specific end-of-life care document.

What have you learned so far by just talking to yourself? This is complicated and requires some real thought. Maybe you need to have more than one self-talk. That's a-okay, because the other thing you've now learned is that these conversations with loved ones will also be complicated. But trust me, you can make it easier than you think, AND you must do it and do it now. If nothing else, Covid-19 has brought to the forefront the need for making clear decisions and having honest conversations about health care issues once and for all.

So, ask yourself:

1. Who do I want in charge of my financial affairs?

2. Who do I want in charge of my health care decisions?

3. Who do I know that I can trust to follow my wishes in end-of-life care?

And after *you* make those decisions, the next step is to have the actual conversation with those people. The most important undertaking here is to get all those documents in place pronto. Note that your Agent under your Financial POA and your Health Care POA and any other person you choose for a DNR, Living Will, etc., does not have to fall on to the shoulders of just one person. You can choose others to share this as Meghan Markle would say, "one loaded piece of toast." Your spouse, of course is usually the first choice, but I have had clients tell me that their husband just cannot make end-of-life decisions or even talk to health care providers and so they chose one of their adult kids, with the blessing of that husband for that one job.

There are situations where someone has chosen three different people to be their financial POA, their Health Care POA and their Living Will Surrogate. One hopes these three people will get along and not end up fighting with each other, but for her reasons, that client wanted to have different people in different jobs with very different responsibilities. I don't know "your people." You do. This is a great time to add, that when a lawyer asks you what seems to be very personal questions about your children and their lifestyle or where they live, it's not because we are writing the next Gossip Girl. We want to get a feel for the people you are putting in charge and also let you know what this job really entails so that you make an informed decision.

I had a mother and daughter both react with raised eyebrows when the mom said her daughter would allow her to come live with the daughter, if anything happened. Her daughter was a nurse, after all. "Nope, Mom, that's not happening," said the nurse. You need to ask your people. Don't assume.

I am always going to tell you to consult with an attorney for these documents, preferably an Elder Lawyer. I know there are dozens of on-line options out there to create these documents in a cheaper way.

I hesitate to completely obliterate that option because these documents are that critical. If that's the only way you will do this, then I begrudgingly relent. But know this: the complexity of the laws surrounding how these documents will ultimately *work,* can leave you or a loved one in a very bad position, especially financially. That's where an attorney who specializes in this work can make all the difference. What is hidden in all that boiler-plate language can be the difference between a spouse or a disabled child becoming *destitute*, or a legacy lost to nursing home costs because the Durable Financial Power of Attorney does not say *exactly* the right thing.

What you spend in several hundred or even just a few thousand dollars to hire an Elder Lawyer to personalize *your* documents for *your* plan, can save hundreds of thousands down the road. An on-line or quickie one-size-fits-all package of legal documents is rarely going to take into account your personal situation especially if you have assets of any kind and by that I mean, a bank account, a 401K, an IRA, a 403B, a house, a spouse, children and a car. If you don't have assets of significance but you are wise enough to know you still want someone you trust to take care of your affairs if something happens to you (and you're not dead, see Plan B), then you can choose a more thrifty course of action. But choose, please choose.

Guardianship

If you don't choose someone, anyone to be in charge if you are sick, incapacitated, and not dead, the next and only path left to help you is Legal Guardianship. If you haven't read about the nightmares of guardianship and you love a good horror story, feel free to Google until you want to light your hair on fire. Guardianship has a place. It's a legal process where you must go to the court, a judge places someone in charge of your affairs both financially and for health care. That person, the guardian, is required to report to the court every penny spent, every decision made and is scrutinized carefully, or is supposed to be. There are all kinds of terrible guardian tales, from relatives to hired guns. But know that even in the best of circumstances where you may have your own spouse as your guardian because you didn't get any Powers of Attorney drawn up and then became incapacitated, you have effectively tied the hands of your spouse to do court-appointed and court-directed things. Remember that gifting thing we talked about up there? Even if you are the guardian of your own spouse, you may be forbidden from "gifting" that spouse's big fat 401k funds to yourself for your mortgage, your annual family beach vacation, or your new roof because your spouse is permanently incapacitated and in a nursing home. It rarely works out well for anyone. So no, don't go there if you can help it. Just choose. And in the words of a great philosopher, "Git 'er done."

C. If I am incapacitated but still in charge, where do I want to live?

Incapacitated may mean many things. It may be that you are just physically unable to live in your current home. If you know that's coming because you have a chronic illness, or bad knees, or you live too far out in the country and won't be able to drive, where do you want to live? There's no reason you can't start looking at the options for later, right now and then discuss that with the people who may need to help you. If you have none of this foreboding baggage, then go to Part D.

The reason this is a conversation you need to have with you is that someone in charge of your affairs may decide to use your money for an over-55 community, assisted living, or home care. Perhaps you would like to think about that in advance. Do you want to live at home and have aides? Do you want to be a burden to your children? Do you want to spend the money to do an in-law suite on your son's house and live there, like you all talked about one day? Do your friends live in a beautiful step-down community where there is ultimately skilled nursing care? Think about these options and have an idea.

D. If I am not incapacitated, where do I want to live?

Do you really want to stay where you are right now? If you're my 93-year-old mom, who was going to the gym and church every day until Covid-19, then the answer is "Yes!" And if we need to battle it out with her one day, we will. But right now, that's her answer. She has the resources and the incredible great health to stay put. There's no question where she wants to live, for now. Is that a question for you? It is, but only you know the answer.

Plan B (for Buried)

I know I said this is a book for sick people, not dead people. But we cannot pretend that we won't be dead and since I have your attention, I thought I would give you a few tips about how to be dead in a really good way.

Powers of Attorney are for live people. Wills are for dead people. Don't ever forget that. Countless people have come up to me after a workshop and said, "I am my mom's executor, so I can take care of all of her paperwork!" Unless your mom is dead you can't legally do her paperwork. This is a point of confusion that exists everywhere. You are not alone, or foolish if you have this misconception. I often think hundreds, nay thousands of years of law has been put in place to confuse rather than enlighten and this is perfect example of that.

Powers of Attorney are for live people who are sick and need help either temporarily or permanently. Wills are for dead people but must be drafted and signed before they become dead.

19

We covered why you need Powers of Attorney in Plan A, now let's talk about wills and how they work and why you might need it.

Wills are actually the easy part about our conversation. Who do I want to give my stuff to when I am dead? Personally, as an Elder Lawyer, I worry less about wills than I do about Powers of Attorney. But lately I've been thinking I should up my worry game, because this is what I'm finding:

Many people have done wills. Many have done them when they were younger, maybe earning some real dough, or buying their first house. Many of you did the "will thing" when you had kids and they were babies and toddlers and you thought, "Gee, who is going to take care of these little angels (or devils) if something happens to us?" Lots of responsible people have wills that are basically *written on papyrus*. How old is that thing? And where is it? And when was the last time you looked at it? Your false sense of security in that document must be crushed. I'm sorry. But if your kids have their own house and car, and you are a grandparent or you bug them every day to make you a grandparent, you need a new will.

Things change. People change. Wills need to change.

Beneficiaries

People get stuff from dead people in a few different ways. One way is as an heir through a will, or as a legally defined heir when someone doesn't leave a will. Yes, the state will decide who gets your stuff, if you don't. And they go through all your long-lost cousins before they take it for themselves, but if *you decide* with a written will then that's who gets your stuff.

There's another really important way people get stuff, usually money, from dead people and that is as a designated beneficiary. Beneficiaries are on life insurance policies, IRAs, 401ks, 403bs, some annuities, some long-term care policies, some credit unions just for being a member, workplace life insurance policies. Beneficiaries are all over the place. If you have any of the things just mentioned, you need to check your beneficiaries right now. Go ahead, I'll wait. Yes, it's that important.

Like I said, things change, people change. Are you in a second marriage? Did you forget to change your work life insurance that you signed 15 years ago? Divorce laws might help you with that, but really? Just check it and fix it. Did you put your daughter and son-in-law on your life insurance and now she's divorced and he is a real creep? Do you need to change that? Do you have a trust for your young children as a beneficiary designation but your kids are now 30 and 32 and you're actually a Grandpa? See what I mean? You need to check every possible place you could have a beneficiary designation and if you have assets, they are out there not just in your will. In fact, generally anything that has a beneficiary designation won't 'go through your will.' What that means is that if you filled out the beneficiary designation the person or persons take that money outright (It does NOT mean there are no tax implications). If you forgot to fill out that beneficiary designation then that money will go to your estate and will pass through your will. Oh, the horror! Oh, the additional possible tax implications! This is why you need a professional. These are labyrinths that are meant to confuse, confound and cost you. And it works merely because we don't check things, especially after things in our lives change.

I would recommend that you check your will and Powers of Attorney at least every five years or if something dramatically changes. And remember that might not be changes to *your life*, it might be to your children's lives, your parents' lives. Some people haven't changed their life insurance since they were 22 and their parents are the beneficiaries, not great if your parents are in a nursing home.

If you are a single person having this conversation with yourself, it should go something like this:

Me: Do I have to think about this now?

Conscience: YES!

Me: Why? I'm _____. Can't it wait? (too young, healthy, busy, don't have the money, watching The Crown)

Conscience: Are you over 18? Then, no, it can't wait. You're a grown-up, act like one.

(Okay, that's not your conscience that's my mother talking to you.)

As a single person, this first chapter gives you questions you need to ask yourself the and then present those answers to an Elder Lawyer for creating the documents that serve your wishes. As a married person, or with a significant other, there is critical information here and, in the chapters, to come. As an adult child or sibling, you, too can find a reason to talk to yourself and then to the person you need to discuss this with besides you!

Now that you have a healthy understanding of the important documents that are needed for long term planning, how are you going to discuss this with the important people in your life? Not just your parents, or any elders you may be in charge of, your adult children, but also your financial advisor and your lawyer and maybe your physician, your pastor, even your bffs. This kind of planning has been shrouded in the dark for too long. We need to get comfortable talking about 'in sickness and in health, "til death do us part," for all of us. So, start your engines, this is going to be fun! Yeah, I said it. Let's have some fun with this!

CHAPTER TWO

A CONVERSTION WITH MY SPOUSE, PARTNER and/or
SIGNIFICANT OTHER

If you are in a relationship, whether you live together or not, you need to have this conversation. And lest you think that you are too young for this, let me assure you there are people, hopefully reading this book, who are in their 20's and 30's who are unpaid, full-time or part-time caregivers and have learned the hard way to have a conversation with significant others about the caregiving journey or aging journey first for their parents or grandparents, and then for themselves.

IF YOU GUYS ARE THE OLD CODGERS:

If you are in your fifth or sixth or seventh or eighth decade of life and you have a significant other who you love, this section is for the two of you to talk turkey about what may lie ahead and how are you prepared to deal with it.

Let's not start with "Honey, we need to talk." How 'bout, "Honey I'm reading this great book, you should read it and then we can talk about it!" Or "Let me read this paragraph to you out of this book!" And then read the information about gifting and 401ks. That gets them every time.

In the alternative, here are a few scenarios that might help start and hopefully continue, not finish this conversation until it's done:

SCENARIO ONE: WHEN YOU ARE ON THE SAME PAGE:

Ted: Hi Honey, I'm home! I just had lunch with the guys and we were talking about _____ and Joe said
(politics, our golf games, retirement)
his wife Darlene took him to _____ where
(the cleaners, the urologist, an Elder Lawyer)
they talked about having all their legal paperwork updated. I think it's time for us to _____ it's been too
(call a lawyer, paint the kitchen, golf)
long since we looked at our old wills. But Joe also talked about POA's. Do we have that?
Anyhow, I got the number of his_____ and
(ELDER LAWYER)
I think we should call her right now and get this done.

Judi: I think that's a great idea! Give me the number I'll make the appointment.

Judi (calling Darlene): Thanks friend, I was so worried about that_____ and I knew if it came from Joe,
(401k, mahjongg, destitution)
we could get this done with an expert! Yes, I'm calling the
_____ now!
(ELDER LAWYER)

As you can see, you may need to enlist some help to get things accomplished, even if you are on the same page. Okay, sometimes it is not this easy. But, sometimes, it is. Sometimes, it is just bringing to the attention of your significant other that you need to have your documents looked at, updated, and refreshed for how your life is going now or may go in the future. If you read any of the 10 million things that clog your newsfeed from AARP you know this topic is critical. There is plenty in the news and all over the internet that you can use to back up your story to have a short, sweet conversation about getting to an Elder Lawyer in your state.

Key Points for when you are on the same page and you're already old (by Millennial standards, so say upwards of 40):

- Do you have POAs, Wills, Living Wills?
- If you do, are they updated or old like you (according to Millennial standards)?
- Are you and/or your partner able to make legal and financial decisions with the appropriate documents according to your state if your significant other is incapacitated?
- Does one spouse or partner have the "Big Kahuna" IRA, 401k, 403b, etc. with all the money in it and the other partner has bupkis? If so, what happens to that money if the owner of the IRA, 401k or 403b becomes incapacitated (note: *not dead*, incapacitated)?
- Have things in your life changed that require a hard look at your health-future? Or the health-future of someone you love who will have an impact on your life?
- Do any of your friends know an Elder Lawyer?
- Did you make an appointment with an Elder Lawyer today, why not?

SCENARIO TWO: WHEN YOU ARE NOT ON THE SAME PAGE

Patty: Honey, we really need to get our_____ done.
(wills, pedicures, family portraits)
Arthur: Stop bugging me. We are not_____ any time soon.

(dying, dancing, looking good)

Patty: Arthur, I am serious. I am worried that_____
(we will get sick, we will lose all our money, all of the above)
_____and if anything happened to
you, I wouldn't be able to handle it and neither would you if
something happened to me. Legally, I mean. Listen to this:

Patty reads passage from 12 CONVERSATIONS:

*More importantly, if you depend on your spouse's retirement
funds to live day-to-day that spouse with the retirement assets
better give you the authority to have access to that 401k or IRA
before she or he is in a coma.*

Arthur: Oh, c'mon. You're being ridiculous. We're fine. We're
healthy and we have no problems. My dad always said, once you do a
will, you're dead. Besides, I'm going out of here in a stretcher, not by
way of a nursing home.

Patty: Now who is being ridiculous? Your Dad died with no
will and it was a disaster with your brothers and sisters. And what if
I'm in a nursing home? Then what? How are YOU going to handle it?

Arthur: You aren't going to any nursing home.

Patty (under her breath): But you might be…

Patty: Listen, Arthur. The kids are coming for dinner tomorrow
night. We are going to talk about these five things and then we or I am
going to a lawyer to get the paperwork done. I want you there. We are
a team. We have been a team for 37 years, and I want us to know what
the other one wants and can do.

Here are the five things Patty and you should discuss with your significant other:

- Who is in charge if something happens to both of us? And by something happens, I mean we are sick, not dead. (Still an important distinction I will continue to drive home.)
- What do we really want if we are truly incapacitated?
  - o Stay at home and get help
  - o Go to a facility
- How will we pay for home help, facility, nursing home?
- How much does it actually cost?
- What happens to the spouse who is not sick? How do they keep the money they need?

Obviously, this can open up a can of worms. Even if you are on the same page these questions need to be addressed. And even going to an Elder Lawyer for the paperwork, may not address all these issues. You can see that other people need to be in on the conversation. Your adult children, your financial advisor, your insurance guy (especially if you have or are considering Long-Term Care insurance in some fashion, which you seriously should at least talk about).

How do we get Arthur off the fence? Here's a few ideas. But ultimately, some Arthurs won't go. It does not mean Patty can't go herself. She can. It is not ideal, but it is part of the solution.

HOW TO GET YOUR SIGNIFICANT OTHER TO THE _____!
(doctor, Elder Lawyer, podiatrist)
- Ask for help
  Sometimes you need to let your partner know that you are asking for help because you are concerned, frightened or

have anxiety about these, or any other issues. When you frame the conversation as a plea for help, you are willingly asking for assistance and not creating an ultimatum.

- Listen to their objections

Arthur's objections about dying if he makes a will, and that he is never going to a nursing home are the exact objections I have heard from spouses more times than I can count. It is not just a comedy routine. Usually, these objections are found to really mean some of the following:

- o It will cost too much to go to a lawyer

Call the lawyers office and get an idea of the cost. Tell them your partner won't come unless you at least have an idea of the cost. You may get, "it depends" from the lawyer, but you can say you only need a ball park to get this started and these documents are too important to ignore. Call another lawyer if you don't like what you hear.

- o I don't think it's *that important*

Here's where your research matters. Find the source that your partner trusts: AARP, his best friend, his golfing buddies, whoever or whatever resource he quotes to you, I guarantee you his trusted sources are talking about retirement, estate planning, nursing home costs, wills, powers of attorney, guardianships. It's in *Forbes, Wall Street Journal, Field and Stream*, it's everywhere. Your partner trusts you, but believes other sources. Use them.

- o What's the rush?

How to create urgency? Well, the easiest way is if you had a friend or relative go through a crisis that was disastrous because they had no paperwork in place.

Quite frankly, there are even movies on Netflix now about the issues with aging, money, and what happens if you are not prepared. It's easy to create urgency with disaster stories. It may be easier to understand urgency just by saying let's get it done for peace of mind, if not your partner's, yours. Not one person knows when they will get hit by a bus, felled by sudden illness, or fall down a flight of stairs. You-know-what *happens*. Urgency is a crisis we are trying to prevent.

Here's how Patty and Arthur might be able to come together:

Patty: Arthur, let's watch that Netflix movie: *I Care A Lot*. I heard from Barb and Tony that it's pretty good.

Arthur: if Tony can watch a movie with Barb that he likes, I'm in.

THE NEXT DAY (and by the way, timing is everything. If you're going to have a conversation with your partner, make sure they aren't tired, hangry (yes, I said 'hangry' that means hungry and angry), upset about the lawn mower, or talking to the grandkids on FaceTime, be conscious and respectful).

Patty: Wow, that movie last night was something, wasn't it?

Arthur: Yeah, thank God, we have each other to look after.

Patty: Yeah, a stranger in charge of our money, if we get sick would be so scary to me.

Arthur: Well, we don't have to worry about that, we are good and we have the kids, too.

Patty: Well, Tony told Barb that he isn't sure his kids are smart enough to handle his money.

Arthur: Ha! He would say that!

Patty: Art, I've been reading this book, (aka *THIS book!)* And after that movie and talking to Barb and Tony, I really think we need to do a few things, just to get our paperwork in order. You know, our wills, our Powers of Attorney, stuff like that.

Arthur: Didn't we do that when the kids were little?

Patty: Yeah, that's the thing. They aren't little and we have other ideas about our retirement. Let's just call Tony and ask who they went to for the legal paperwork, okay?

Arthur: Can we afford that?

Patty: Barb will tell me how much she paid. Or I will just call a few law offices and see what it costs. It's really important. That movie got me shook up a bit. I want to decide who takes care of our money and our decisions if anything happens to us. We have so many friends who have to take care of their parents, with nursing home costs and who knows what. It scares me. Please help me feel better about this, Art.

Arthur: Okay, well figure it out and let me know what you find out. Then we will talk about it.

The door can be opened. One, or both of you can do the homework here to find out why it's important and what questions you need to ask. It can be done, my friends.

SCENARIO THREE: WHEN YOU ARE TOO YOUNG TO HAVE THIS CONVERSATION

> Heather: Hey hon, my mom and dad want us to come for dinner and talk about their retirement.

> Jake: Why do we need to talk about *their* retirement?

> Heather: I think it's because they got some bad news. My Dad may have Alzheimer's Disease.

> Jake: Oh my God, Heather! I am so sorry. That's terrible. Okay, well what does that mean? I mean, what are they going to do? And what does that mean for us? And wow, oh my God. This is just...I don't know, it's just terrible.

> Heather: Yeah, it really is.

Heather and Jake have just entered the Twilight Zone. You see, the conversation is about her parents and his in-laws, but ultimately (and we will address this in the next few Chapters because it has so many permutations), what would be a good result from this is that Heather and Jake recognize that they, too, need to do some planning for themselves. Right here and right now.

There is no way Heather and Jake will come out of this experience unscathed. They will be called upon in some fashion to help. At least, we hope so. This is what family does. But for purposes of "conversations," ideally Heather and Jake will not only help her parents, they will take some action to help themselves.

This is what should happen very shortly thereafter:

Heather: You know, Jake, now that we got Mom and Dad squared away with their paperwork, their plan for if and/when they will need help and looked at the cost of all this, I'm thinking we need to so some planning ourselves.

Jake: Heather, we are in our 40's. We're fine. Let's just get through this with your Mom and Dad.

Heather: Jake, really? I mean. I am so scared. What if something happens to you? Or me? What if I get this disease? Or geez, what if the stress of it makes us sick, or my mom and I have to quit our jobs? I mean there is so much here. Don't you think we should at least get our wills, and Powers of Attorney? I mean something could happen to us tomorrow, then what?

Jake: We can't afford that, Heather.

Heather: We can't afford what? Getting sick? Needing help? Helping my parents?

Jake: A lawyer, Heather. We can't afford a lawyer.

Heather: Well, we will ask how much it cost my parents, and we will call around, and at worst we will do the internet thing. We can't afford not to have this done, Jake. I'm looking at Mom and Dad and I see what we can't afford and being unprepared is the worst.

As we go through the next chapters, remember what you are trying to accomplish here. It's not about being right, nagging, getting the upper hand or even scaring people (although I find that scaring people has some real heft...not like Freddy Kruger scaring, but like "Holy cow, I did NOT KNOW THAT?!?"

If some of the chapters do not apply to you that's okay, but I would ask that you do not skip the chapters on talk to your lawyer and your financial advisor. Even if you don't have those experts on your team yet, you may want to. If you do have those people on your team, you are going to learn about why it is so important for them to be in a conversation with *each other and you*. Once you get everyone on the same page as to your plan for incapacity or death you can rest easy, at least until things change, or a crisis occurs, or the sky is falling...but look how prepared you will be!

CHAPTER THREE

A CONVERSTION WITH MY PARENTS

In some ways, this could be the hardest conversation. There is so much baggage between parents and adult children. We take our five-year-old selves to every holiday, funeral, birthday party and family dinner when we are with our parents. Even in the best of relationships, parent/child navigation is always going to have "The Perfect Storm," moments. Therefore, we will walk softly and carry a big stick!

True stories from my own life:

Me: Mom, we probably should go pre-pay your funeral. It's one of those expenses that if you get sick and end up in any kind of long-term care, you can pay in advance and there is no penalty for doing it, if we need Medicaid in the future to help pay for a nursing home.

My Mom: Okay.

It looks like that was easy. That conversation was at least five years ago and nothing has happened. Over these last five years we talked about who should go to the funeral home to help decide so that there would be no battles with my seven siblings or their families. We talked about which funeral home makes you look the nicest in your casket. We talked about how much to spend. We talked about what kind of casket. We talked about what music she would like. My mom told me she has a book where you can put all this information. This is how that went:

My Mom: I have a book where I can put all of that information about what I want for my funeral.

Me: That's great.

Me: (because I know my mom): Did you actually put anything in that book?

My Mom: No.

And here we are. I am no stranger to these conversations having been a caregiver for aunts, great aunts, a mother-in-law, my own mother, a brother-in-law, and a best friend. And I have failed to get some things done because of lack of cooperation. But it doesn't mean I haven't tried. And I have tons of family members and friends who still haven't heard my message. Well, they've heard it, they just haven't listened. So, I get it. But we are going to keep trying in your family because I'm doing this for you. If you are going to end up as a caregiver, like I did at least 8 times already, I want you to have every fighting chance you can, and parents are one of the first fights you will probably have. The bell has rung and this is round one!

THE BASIC CONVERSATION:

Howard: Mom, Dad we need to talk.

Mom: Oh, Howard, what now? We're fine. Or is it you? Do you need help? Are you okay? Are you sick?

Howard: No Mom, I'm fine. I want to talk about making sure all your paperwork is in order.

Dad: What paperwork? Like taxes?

Howard: No, Dad, like wills and Powers of Attorney and Living Wills.

Dad: Oh that. Your mother takes care of that.

Mom: No, I don't. Well, I did that one time, when we picked Uncle Sol and Aunt Mimi for your guardians if we died when you and your sister were in grade school.

Dad: See, Howie, we're good.

Howard: You are not GOOD, Dad. That's not good. You need to do this stuff now.

Mom: Oh, we're fine. You'll take care of it, Howard.

Howard: That's what I'm trying to do, Mom, take care of it. We need to go to the lawyer's office. But before we do, we need to talk about what happens if one of you gets sick. How are we going to handle that?

Dad: What? We get sick, we go to the hospital, we either come home or die. What's to talk about?

Howard: Dad. It doesn't always work that way.

Mom: He's right, honey. Remember Sol, he had that stroke and Mimi was going to the nursing home every day. Nearly killed her.

Dad: Sol's a putz. He smoked, he drank, he sat. We don't do that.

Howard: That's the guy you picked to be our guardian?!

Dad: What? He had a nice business, a nice house. You would've been fine, maybe lucky even.

Mom: Your cousins are fine. They didn't do so bad. Maybe you should ask them for a job for your son.

Howard: Mom, Dad this is not the point or why we are here. Wait a minute, my son is fine he works for the FBI. What's wrong with my son?

It can go south, so quickly. Try to stay focused. This is where a lawyer could help. There would be less talk about Uncle Sol, not completely, I assure you, but less.

Mom: Your son is fine, it's just he's never home. He doesn't visit so much anymore.

Howard: Okay, Mom, Dad we are going to the lawyer. I will take you there next week and we will get the important papers updated or even started. You're in your eighties, it's time to make this right.

Dad: Okay, but don't make it Monday, that's when I have breakfast with my bowling buddies.

Mom: And Tuesday is mahjongg so Tuesday is out.

Howard: Fine next week, not Monday or Tuesday.

Howard learned quickly, or maybe over 50 years, that he should just let the lawyer handle it. This has become a great strategy for the parents of many of my clients. Any lawyer worth her salt will talk to your parents without you in the room. While gathering facts you can be there, but the nitty gritty of what your parents want should be discussed privately, by your parents with the attorney. Once that is done, the attorney can invite you back in to discuss with you whatever your parent wishes. I took my own mother to an attorney to create her will so that everyone knows it was a private consultation without my influence. Even if you are an only child, it should still be private until your parent gives the lawyer permission to share with you. That is not to say there are not exceptions to every rule. Your mom or dad are the final deciders, so if they insist that you be there at all times because they are intimidated by the process, you are the only heir they have, they have their reasons, then the lawyer can memorialize that in a memo in her file. You can even ask her to do that.

THE BASIC CONVERSTATION WHEN ONLY ONE PARENT IS LISTENING:

Parents are no different than you and your spouse, and so one of them might be on board to listen but the other may reject every attempt you make to do the basic paperwork. As you go through this chapter, you will begin to understand that although this basic paperwork is critical, it is the tip of the iceberg, and we are on the Caregiving Titanic.

What does one do if only one parent will even listen? There can be several approaches and several conversations. Some of the same tools that we talked about in Chapter One such as using outside influencers that your reluctant Mom or Dad trusts more than you, whether it be real people, like your rich Uncle Sol or the Women's Day magazine in the grocery store check-out line are always available to you. Using professionals including not only your parents' lawyer, or better yet an Elder Lawyer, but also your parents' doctor, pastor or accountant are also good options.

If you only have one member of the parent team on your side, then the best thing to do is begin with listening. Listen as to why your other parent objects. Listen hard and between the lines. The objections that "I don't need anything because I am just going to die," often really means, "This is scary and I don't want to talk about it." This is especially true as you get older and frailty is on the horizon if not right here. If you hear, "What do you know? You're just a kid," it means you're my kid and I'm the adult here so don't tell me what to do.

We could come up with a million scenarios, but instead let's look at a way to talk to and convince one parent and see how that might influence the other parent.

Five Things:

1. Ask questions and then listen:
    - Ask if they have any of these documents: Will, POA, Living Will, Advanced Directive, Five Wishes, etc., and if they do have these documents, ask if you can see them.
    - Ask them if they have considered what will happen if one of them gets seriously ill.
    - Ask them where you fall in that scenario. What do they expect of you? (and btw, don't react like a maniac when they say they are living with you, if that's not your plan…you are listening, remember?).

    Write down what you hear. Later you can use this as a guide, as a reminder to him/her, or as ammunition if you need to! Writing it down gives you pause, helps you listen and helps to get a plan on paper.

This is a great opportunity to ask the agreeable parent why they think their spouse is not on board just to talk. You may get some insight. Timing is everything, try to do this when you have time and space to be together comfortably.

2. Bring Information to the table:

Reading this and taking some tidbits from here is homework. You may also look into facilities around town that you believe they might like, if that's part of your concern. Or you may look into the cost of home care or things like that. If your concerns are immediate and bigger than just getting legal documents done, the more information you have, the more civil the conversation can be. Make it informative, not demanding. If one conversation is about paperwork and that's it for the day, make the information conversation for next time. You have to proceed with caution and pace it so that you are not overwhelming either parent.

3. Be kind:

Do not get up in their grills, as the kids say. Yes, we both know this is for you as much as it is for them. But being forceful, adamant and a know-it-all never helped anyone, especially in the parent-child relationship. Just ask your parents. That being said, go back to Number 1. Listen, be kind and try to ask questions. Then give them the answers about why you are concerned, a bit frightened, and looking to give everyone peace of mind here before there is a big problem.

4. Involve your siblings and/or your spouse:

If you have siblings, or you have a partner, they have to be a part of this. Everyone here will be involved or should be if something goes awry, and so they should be in the loop. If your wife has a great relationship with your mom, like I was lucky enough to have with my precious mother-in-law, then your wife should be included, especially if we all know she is going to be doing the heavy lifting. Let's not kid ourselves here. Help is not a classic four-letter word, but it is treated as such in the caregiving world and we need to stop that right now. Involve those who are to be involved from the get-go.

5. Have action steps at the end of every conversation:

Like my mom and the funeral prep, we keep talking about what she wants, so we do have some action steps. We haven't gone to the funeral home, Covid-19 took care of that, but we do know some things. If you can get your mom to agree to talk to your dad by Friday about going to the lawyer next week, that is a win. If you can get your dad to agree to let you see his old will to see if needs to be updated, also a win. You have to have action even if it's baby steps.

So how might this go?

Howard: Mom, I know Dad doesn't want to talk about important things like going to a lawyer and getting Powers of Attorney and new wills done, but I am so worried about both of you if you get sick and need help. Even I can't help you completely if I don't have the legal power to do so.

Mom: I know, son. I know.

Howard: Do you have any ideas or suggestions?

Mom: Well, let me see. I could ask your Dad's best friend what are they doing? He comes home every week with what Ben is doing and how we should do that, whatever it is.

Howard: That's a good idea! Can you talk to Ben by Friday? I'm coming over this weekend and maybe we can use the conversation with Ben as a help to make an appointment with a lawyer, maybe even Ben's lawyer.

Mom: Okay. That's a good idea.

Howard: Mom, have you and Dad ever talked about what happens if either of you get sick?

Mom: Well, I try. But he doesn't like to go there.

Howard: How 'bout you? What are you thinking?

Mom: Well, I know my friends Jane and Carla are really happy over at Arbor Square. And, oh my God, Howard, it is just beautiful. Have you seen that place? No, I guess not. But it's gorgeous. But I doubt we can afford that. Although, I have no idea how Jane and Carla can afford it, I mean we were neighbors for forty years.

Howard: Wow, I had no idea you looked at a place like that? Did you really like it? Did Dad go with you?

Mom: No, I was just visiting my friends. But I did tell him how gorgeous it was and how good the food was. But he said we don't have money for a hoity-toity place like that.

Howard: Let me do some homework on that Mom, okay?

Mom: Sure. It's just so beautiful, Howie. And no grass to cut, no snow to shovel. I mean it would be so nice.

This all comes as a surprise to Howard. So, listen up, people. Do some research. Baby steps and you too, may make some headway with one or both of your parents.

I will admit here and now that there will be times of frustration and lack of progress (see funeral home conversation). You have to decide which of those issues you can live with in terms of lack of progress. If you are in a real crisis; dementia has gone on too long; Dad keeps falling and Mom tries to pick him up; Mom, the healthy parent, is now hospitalized because taking care of Dad has become too much for her. If you are there, then you will likely be forced to take some immediate action. Of course, if you have been talking about these things for weeks, months or years, your chosen course of "crisis" action may not be that surprising to you or your parents even though you haven't put everything in place that you wanted to, in advance. That's why the conversations are so important. It's like those old Public Service Announcements: "The More You Know..."

The next chapters are just Mom and Dad alone. This may seem redundant, but research shows that men and women react to these issues very differently. If your parent is widowed the conversations have a different twist and I believe it is beneficial to take Mom and Dad separately to recognize that they may be looking at things from a point of view that is different from what you might expect.

CHAPTER FOUR

A CONVERSATION WITH MOM

Mom is single. She is either divorced or widowed or was never married. The important thing is that she is single, getting older, and you will be the one she calls on for help. It may be that she is helping you now, but that can change on a dime, so *both* of you are likely looking at each other with worry and anxiety.

Mom will always worry about you. She may or may not know that you are just as worried about her. The first step towards peace of mind is getting those legal documents done. When you are dealing with a single person, or you are a single person who has not chosen who will step up for you in a crisis, you are already in the pre-crisis stage. Mom has got to get that helper in place. Like Mr. Rogers says, "Look for the helpers." But those helpers can't help if Mom hasn't given the authority to do so in writing. Financial institutions and hospitals are buggers for legal authority, don't waste another day pretending that you can help Mom. She will need help and you need to ask her not to tie the hands of her helper by not doing the requisite paperwork so you and her financial person, insurance person or any other person can do their job.

The conversations may be similar to what we've already discussed. But as conversations can go so many ways, let's look at the day before you are getting in the car to go to the lawyer. You've already accomplished the following (if not, this is a good checklist):

1. Had "the talk" about why Power of Attorney, Wills and Living Wills are important.

    Maybe even watched: *I Care A Lot* on Netflix or *The Father* or *Elizabeth is Missing* or *The End* on Showtime, whatever it takes.

2. Decided who in the family would be in charge of Mom's finances and who would be in charge of Mom's health care decisions.

3. Decided what Mom wants to do if she is in a permanent vegetative state (You might call it a permanent coma since no one likes the word "vegetative," but that's what lawyers use all the time).

4. Picked the right lawyer who does this kind of work.

5. Discussed with other family members if appropriate.

6. Put the date and time on Mom's calendar and reminded her incessantly about where you are going and when.

7. Arrive early enough so that you can make sure Mom is ready to go. If she is, great, go get a coffee. If she isn't you won't be frustrated before you even leave the house.

You arrive at Mom's house. Away we go! Not so fast…

Mom: Oh hi, Jenny! What are you doing here?
    (Mom does not have dementia; she is playing you)

Jenny: Mom, you know we are going to the lawyer today.
Mom: Oh, is that today?

Jenny: Well, looks like you're ready to go somewhere, so that's wonderful. Let's get your coat and get on the road.

Mom: Oh, I don't know Jenny. Have you discussed this with your brother?

Jenny: Yes, in fact we both did. Mom, what's the problem? Why are you hesitant?

Mom: I don't know, it feels so final. It feels like I won't be in charge anymore.

Jenny: Oh, Mom. I totally understand. We are going to try as hard as we can to let you   know you are in control. It's your money, your health decisions, all yours. This is only if anything happens and you need help.

Mom: Great. Then you do the same.

Jenny: Do the same what?

Mom: You talk to the lawyer about your documents. Who will be in charge if anything happens to you? Who will make decisions if you need help? See?

Jenny: Wow, Mom, you are right. I'll talk to them today while we are there to set up my own appointment.

Out of the mouths of Baby Boomers.

Now you and Mom and everyone in your family are on board with Mom's documents. Does it end there? Not really. There are a few more conversations you should have and then perhaps you can do the *Frozen* thing and "let it go."

The financial, insurance and health care conversations will follow in those chapters. But what if Mom is adamant that she will not cooperate. She is not going to a lawyer, she won't sign any documents, she is going to remain in her house in control of her affairs and no one is going to change her mind.

Here are some options:

Karl: Mom, there's a few things we need to_____.
                        (talk about, throw out, disinherit)
Mom: Okay, honey. I'm just glad you're finally here spending time with me.

Karl: Mom, I come here every Sunday.

Mom: I know, but it's nice to sit and talk about something important. What is it we need to talk about?

Karl: Mom, I want to take you to the lawyer and get your paperwork updated.

Mom: No. What else can we talk about? Your sister? Your wife? Your awful neighbors? Your questionable job? J Lo's newest main squeeze?

Karl: Mom, stop deflecting. Hey, what's wrong with my job? Wait, no, Mom we're going to discuss this.

Mom: No, Karl. Nobody is in charge but me.

Karl: Mom, who have you been talking to?

Mom: Everyone and no one.

Karl: Mom, I'm just trying to help.

Mom: I don't need any help. You think coming one day a week means "help?"
I take care of myself just fine, thank you very much.

Karl: I know that. And I don't want to change any of that. I just want to be able to help if you need it.

Mom: No. I'll tell you when I need it.

Karl: Okay, but here's the thing. What if you can't tell me? What if you fall down the stairs carrying the laundry, like you do every Tuesday? Not fall down the stairs, but doing the laundry. Or what if you are in a car accident on the way to the hairdresser and you can't talk to me? I mean there's all kinds of crazy drivers out there, you don't know who is taking your safety in their hands.

Mom: Well...

Karl: Can I at least go to the doctor's office with you and tell them to call me if you need me?

Mom: Yes, you can come to Dr. Wang's office with me.

This is when you are going to call the doctor's office the week before you go and ask to speak to the doctor or put a note in your mother's file that you are enlisting the doctor's help to get your mother to sign a Health Care Power of Attorney and Living Will.

Karl: And I want to sit down with you and Kara to talk about what you want Mom.

This is how you are changing the phrasing. It is just about what Mom wants and that could be anything. It doesn't talk about you being in charge or taking away her decision-making power. Make sure your call with Kara is at a time when everyone has time to calmly and pleasantly discuss just, "what happens in a crisis?" Phrase it as a temporary band-aid when Mom might be sick for a short time. And it is, and should be about listening to what Mom wants in a crisis. Ultimately, the goal is to get paperwork in place AND to recognize how you can make Mom less scared and more comfortable with "what if..."

Mom: How are we going to do that? She lives in Hawaii!

Karl: We have the internet now, Mom. The same way you talk to Kara and her kids, we can talk about important things, too.

Mom: I don't want to do that. People might hear us!

Karl: It's okay, Mom. We won't tell any secrets. We will just get a general idea about what to do if you need us in an emergency.

Mom: Okay, I guess.

When you finally do get to make the call with your sibling, here is a way to discuss this without being threatening and yet, hopefully accomplish some goals.

Talk about the following:
Legal:

1. Does Mom have an attorney that she knows or that her friends have recommended to do the paperwork. You should have an attorney at the ready so that you can bring up the attorney's website for everyone to see.
2. See what day is best to make an appointment for Mom and then schedule it. As soon as you hang up, or if it's the weekend do it first thing Monday morning. *Action steps, now.*
3. Does everyone agree about who will be in charge and how that will work? If Mom's children live far apart, can the long-distance child have input, authority, or responsibility of any kind? What will that be? And for heaven's sake, be practical.
4. If and it is a BIG IF, Mom needs long-term care, ideally what would she want to do? You think you know the answer, and you may be right, but ask her anyway. Her ability to have input is important to your listening. We, elders are not dead here, we are trying to be responsible, but don't forget Aretha said it best: R-E-S-P-E-C-T!

Financial:

1. Does Mom have a financial advisor? Does she need one? If so, have you done your homework before this meeting to have a choice of two for her? If not, who is going to handle the finances? Will you do it as a POA and/or joint bank account owner? This needs to be discussed with the lawyer as there is a big difference in these two ways to handle finances and it has far-reaching legal implications for Medicaid and for inheritance.

2. If Mom does have a financial advisor, one of you should go with Mom to an appointment. You need to meet her financial advisor and let her financial advisor know you are Mom's POA in case of emergency. Make the appointment.

Medical:

1. Who is/are Mom's physicians? You should get a list and you should go to an appointment with her to the important ones. You don't need to go to the dentist or the eye doctor if Mom only goes for regular check-ups. But you should meet her General Practitioner, her Internist, her critical doctors so that they know you in a crisis.
2. Does Mom need to go to a doctor? If so, make the appointment, even if it is just for a well visit and Mom hasn't gone for years. Then the responsible person is in the loop with the medical decision maker.

That's it. Any more than this is probably too much for the first go-round. There are many more conversations to be had. Right now, our job is to get the ball rolling and get things in place. It may be like a home renovation show. Be prepared to find termites, water damage, mold and pipes that need replacing. You are no doubt opening a can of worms in some fashion. That's the beauty of preparation. You have time to handle it. Whatever information you glean from these first steps you can then move forward with research, experts, and perchance some cooperation from Mom and her legal, financial and medical providers.

To be honest, women are usually much more compliant with taking care of business, especially if they are widows and their adult children are asking for cooperation. But this is not always the case.

When it is not the case, it is either because you are her kid, and she still thinks you don't know anything. Or you are her kid and she thinks this stuff is private adulting stuff. Or she is embarrassed by her circumstances, whatever they may be. Or she is a control freak (I fall into this category) and thinks you are a hot-shot who wants to take control. Or she doesn't trust the system: i.e. lawyers, doctors, etc. Or she doesn't trust *your* partner. Or she never dealt with these issues because your Dad did it all and it is just too overwhelming for her.

If you can't get this far because Mom stays adamant that she is not going to budge. She will not go to a lawyer, doctor, or Lordy Loo, a "financial advisor?!" then I do have a few scare tactics that might work. They involve finding out what is going on with her friends, or relatives that can serve as a cautionary tale. You know, all those stories that your mom tells you when you are on the phone with her and you're not paying attention. You gotta' listen. There's gold in them thar' hills.

Karl: Mom, I heard your best friend Helen is moving to a nursing home.

Mom: Where did you hear that?

Karl: Actually, her son called me to tell me so that you wouldn't call her or drive over there and find her gone. So that was nice. He told me where she will be so we can go visit her there.

Mom: Oh, Helen…

Karl: The worst part is she is going to the county home, Happy Acres.

Mom (snorts): "Happy Acres!" The only thing happy about that place will be when they tear it down.

Karl: I know. It's such a shame, but when Helen's husband got sick, they used up all his money for his care and she just can't afford anywhere else.

Mom: That's terrible.

Karl: Mom...

Mom: What?

Karl: I don't want that to happen to you.

Mom: So, don't put me in shitty acres.

Karl: I won't but you need to help me. You need to get the paperwork done, so I'm in charge. And you need to let me see your finances so we can make sure you're okay.

OR....................

Karl: Mom, Dad died and left you no money.

Mom: WHAT? What are you talking about?

Karl: When Dad died, all of his money was in his IRA. He used that for health care costs in the nursing home, and he didn't have a beneficiary so it went to his estate. We had to distribute it in a way that made us pay a fortune in income tax and that left very little.

Mom: What are you telling me?

Karl: I'm telling you that if Dad had listened to me and done a few things to make it easier on you, we might not be in this predicament. I need you to go with me to the lawyer and financial advisor so that we can set you up to be comfortable, especially if we have a crisis like we did with Dad and his stroke.

Mom: No.

Karl: Yes.

Mom: No.

Karl: What will it take for you to go with me?

Mom: I don't know.

Karl: That's a good start. Do you want to go_____?
(on Tuesday, with a friend too, before it's too late?)

Mom: No.

Karl: Are you afraid of_____?
(losing control, you don't know the lawyer, you will end up like Dad?)

Karl: Do you want to talk to_____?
(another family member, a friend, your doctor, your pastor?)

Karl: What's the best day for us to go to_____?
(your lawyer, your doctor, your pastor, your friend, lunch?)

Karl: Mom, I know this is uncomfortable. But we are not going to make the same mistakes we made with Dad, okay? For your safety and peace of mind, we are going to start this week to make some appointments.

Speaking of Dad...

CHAPTER FIVE

A CONVERSATION WITH DAD

Oh, Dad.

Dads are different from Moms. Yes, they are your parents. But often their focus is quite distinct when it comes to preserving what is important to them. Be aware we are talking about everything from money, homes, driving privileges, and decisions about moving, to high-concept ideas like dignity, respect, a legacy, fear, and security for themselves and each other. The concrete things seem to present obvious solutions. It is those intangibles that get us all into trouble when having these important conversations. It would seem almost impossible to create a template for working through this quickly and efficiently, not because the questions aren't clear, but because the drivers behind the answers may be foggy even to Dad. He doesn't know why he doesn't want to do these things; he just knows he doesn't want to. But as my Nana says, "You can wish in one hand and spit in the other and see which gets filled first!" Meaning, you have to do something, you can't wish it away and you are the doer. So how DO we get Dad to be our co-doer?!?

Son: Dad, ever since Mom died, you've been getting a little dodgy.

Dad: I'm fine.

Son: Okay. But even being 'fine,' can we just go over a few things in case you get to a point where you aren't fine?

Dad: What kind of things?

Son: Like do you have a Power of Attorney or a recent will?

Dad: A Power of Attorney? Who do you think I am, Rockefeller? And my will is just fine.

Son: Dad, I'm guessing you leave everything to Mom, so it's not fine. Plus, a Power of Attorney isn't for rich people. It's for people who need help if they are sick, even if they are sick just for a short time and can't pay their bills.

Dad: Well...

Son: Dad, I can't pay your bills for you without authority. I can't make sure your checks coming in can be deposited. I can't do anything.

Dad: Well, why not?

Son: Because the bank, Social Security, your financial guy, none of them will talk to me without a Power of Attorney. And, honestly, Dad they shouldn't, unless you say it's okay.

Dad: Well then, I'll just say it's okay when I need to.

Son: Dad...

Dad: Son…

Son: Dad, suppose you had a stroke like Uncle Henry, or dementia like Mom. How could I help you then? You were so adamant that only you could help Mom. Thank God, everything you had was jointly owned or that could have been a nightmare. Now that we have lived through that experience, I can see the writing on the wall, and it's not good, Dad. We need to get this paperwork done and we need to get some kind of simple plan in case anything happens to you.

Dad: Am I in charge of my money and my house? Am I in charge of where I live and what I do?

Son: Yes, Dad. You are. This is only if you need my help. What if you can't talk or walk like Uncle Henry? I would have to go to court and get a guardianship for you because Mom isn't here anymore. Please Dad. Help me. This could be fine, or it could get very bad. Very, very bad.

Dad: Son, I'll take care of it.

Son: No, Dad you won't. Mom has been gone for three years now. It's time. Please, I'm really concerned. I promise not to overstep. If I do, you can tell me. We can have a safe word. How about that? If I'm going too far, or you don't like what's happening, how about you say, "Phillies!" and I'll know we need to take a break or dial it back? Can we do that?

Dad: Okay.

Son: Dad, I'm calling the lawyer now. We are going to make the appointment now, okay? We have to commit to this.

Dad: Phillies!

Son: DAD!

Dad: See, you already can't take criticism.

Son: Dad, really? I mean do you really mean Phillies right now?

Dad: Nah, I just wanted to see what you would do.

Son: Okay, then. I'm calling now. Get your calendar out.

Now let's pretend this is not going to go well. Some of you are saying, "Pretend?!?"

Son: Dad, we need to talk. You are falling apart here since Mom died and we have to get some things organized.

Dad: Is that why you came here? To criticize and abuse me?

Son: Oh my God, Dad! I'm trying to help.

Dad: Some kind of help that is!

Son: Okay, okay. You're right. Let me start over. Dad, I would like to take you to the lawyer's office to get your paperwork updated in case something happens to you. And I'd also like to help with your bank accounts.

Dad: That's much better. Thank you, Son, but no.

Son: DAAAAAD!

Dad. Seriously, I'm fine.

Son: You're not fine and even if you were fine, I'm not fine. What will I do if something happens like a stroke, or a fall, or whatever and I don't have the paperwork to help you?

Dad: Nothing is going to happen to me.

Son: Seriously, Dad. Which god are you now? How do YOU know that? Geez. You have friends, brothers and even Mom who didn't go gently into that good night. C'mon Dad. Help me out here.

Dad: I'm going to live in my house and die in my sleep.

Son: Oh, for God's sake! Really? Ok. Let's play that game. It's three A.M., you have to get up to pee. You stumble to the bathroom as usual, but this time you trip over who-knows-what and fall. You can't get up and you don't have your phone handy so you lie there until morning until you can see to crawl across the room to the phone. But you didn't fall, you had a mini-stroke because you won't give up your damn stogies and that doesn't mix well with your high blood sugar and your nightly scotch. Do I have this about right?

Dad: You're just making things up.

Son: Which things are made-up, Dad?

Dad: The thing about falling.

Son: Exactly, everything else is a real possibility. So, hear me out. The ambulance comes and they call me and I rush to the hospital. They say: "Your Dad broke his wrist, he needs surgery, but he's so dehydrated he really is incoherent. Are you his Health Care Power of Attorney? No? Oh, geez that's too bad. Who is? No one? Yikes!"

Dad: That's ridiculous!

Son: Is it? I mean is it really?

Dad: Well, not that ridiculous, I suppose.

Son: Oh, there's more. You broke your wrist so you can't sign your checks to pay your bills. You will be in rehab for about 10 days for physical therapy and no one can pay your bills because you have given none of your children access to your bank accounts or even where your damn checkbook is. So, all your bills are late or overdue and it's bs.

Dad: Okay, okay, I get your point.

Son: Do you? Do you, Dad?

This isn't going exactly as planned. Or it is...for Dad.

Son: Okay, Dad. Just tell me this. What are your objections to letting me help out if you need me?

Dad: None. I'll let you know when I need you.

Son: Ugh. That's the problem what if you can't let me know, and then you need me?

Dad: Kid, I got this.

Son: Dad, please. Just go with me to the lawyer. If you don't want to sign any papers then fine. How about that?

Dad: Hmmmm.

Son: I'll take you out for breakfast or lunch. We will go to the lawyer's office. You can talk to her and then decide if you will do anything or nothing. How about that? After all, the lawyer is the expert, not me.

Dad: I'm not spending any money on a damn lawyer.

You can go two ways here:

Son: Okay, I'll pay for the visit. If you decide to hire her, then it's your cost.

OR:

Son: Okay, I'll pay for it, how about that?

Dad: You'll pay for it? You can't afford it!

Son: I can't afford not to. If you fall down what am *I* going to do?

Dad: So, this is all about you?

Son: Oh, Dad. Okay, yeah, it's about me. I'm your kid and I need your help.

Dad: Well, as long as you understand that...and you pay. Fine.

There is so much going on here, isn't there? Old patterns, old arguments, old people. It's a lot to digest. But there is some psychology going on here, too. There is an underlying method to Son's madness. He is, whether aware of it or not, using scare tactics, please-help-me tactics, what-do-you-really-object-to tactics, I'll-take-you-out-to-lunch-and-spend-time-with-you tactics, I'll-pay-for-it tactics and finally, you-are-so-right tactics. All of these can help you. What will likely not help you is yelling, arguing strongly or insisting you are right no matter what...even if you are. I know this because I'm right and everyone always wants to argue with me!

So here are the eight things we learned here:

1. Take them to an expert to handle their objections.
2. Find out what is really bugging them.
3. Can you bribe them? It worked with you when you were a toddler!
4. Will you help me? Get him to help you.
5. Are you scared, Dad?
6. Do you actually understand what happens if you get sick?
7. How about spending time with me, Dad? (also, a bribe but also a Harry Chapin "Cat's in the Cradle" idea. If you don't know what I'm talking about, Google it, it's important.)
8. Tell me what *you* think about you getting sick.

How do we make both of you right and by that I mean get the job done without gloating? The gloating thing only applies to you, not Dad. He gets all the gloating rights he wants if the deed gets done.

I might add that practicing with someone is not a bad idea. If you and your brother or sister know how your dad is going to react, do a simulation with each other. See if one of you can convince the one who is playing "Dad" to take the action you need. Based on what you know about your dad, you could probably easily figure out his usual objections. Since you are his kids, you may know some of his soft spots to use as tools to help move this conversation and action along. At the very least, you may get him to a lawyer or let you look at his important papers, or whatever the challenge is that you are facing. Start somewhere. Plus, if you Tik-Tok the simulation it you might become a viral sensation!

CHAPTER SIX

A CONVERSATION WITH MY ADULT CHILDREN

This may seem like we have already discussed this considering we talked to Mom and Dad both together and separately, but that was from the kid's perspective. What about you, Mom and/or Dad? What about your concerns that your kids are ignoring aging issues, brushing under the carpet or don't want to talk about you getting older because you will handle it and they just can't? Do they know how you want to handle it? Are they going to be on board with you? Do you have expectations of your adult children that you have not expressed? Do they have expectations that you do not want to engage with? Hmmmm. This calls for some coffee and conversation. And I wouldn't say no to a little coffee cake, either. It may be a while!

WHEN SUZY COMES FOR COFFEE

Mom: Hi Suzy!

Suzy: Hi Mom, what's up? You said you wanted to talk to me about something important?

Mom: Yes, not tragic, get that look off your face. Just important.

Suzy: Okay, hahaha, where's the coffee?

Mom: Grab yourself a cup and I made a nice vegan coffee cake. Help yourself. I cannot believe how delicious it actually is!

Suzy: Mom! Oh boy, vegan cake...(Suzy is impressed, so will your grandkids be!)

Mom: I have all kinds of surprises still left in me. I'm not dead yet!

Suzy: Mom! Stop!

Mom: Oh, Suzy, take a joke, will you, please? It's Saturday, the sun is shining, let's just have a nice chat.

Suzy: Okey dokey, and good cake, by the way!

Mom: Right? Anyway, I want to talk about my will and also what happens to me if I get sick.

Suzy: Mom!
Mom: It's fine Suzy. Not enough people are talking about this. My friend, Joan is in a nursing home now because she fell in her own house going up and down those damn stairs doing the laundry and nobody ever discussed what she would want. I'm sick of that happening to my friends and their kids making decisions without ever asking their parents what they want. So, I am going to tell you and I am going to write it down so everyone knows we talked about this.

Suzy: Okay, okay. Let's do this.

Mom: Okay.

At the end of the chapter, we will talk about how to write down what you need or want. In the meantime, while we're eavesdropping in the middle of a good dialogue, let's hear how Suzy and Mom tackle this:

Mom: I want you to know that I love you and your brother very much.

Suzy: Oh, Mom (brushing a tear from her eye).

Mom: Suzy we will never get through this if you keep saying, 'Oh, Mom!'

Suzy just looks at her.

Mom: I love you and I want what's best for you. You know I took care of Nana and Poppy for a long time. I don't want that for you. But I also don't want to be housed like a forgotten old shoe.

Suzy: Mom, you know we love you.

Mom: And I know you have busy lives and fun lives and kids and I don't want you missing out on any of that. But that being said, know that my money will go to my care. Yes, I want to unburden you and your brother, but I also want you to know that your father and I raised and educated you both at great expense to be self-sufficient. So, our money will go to our care first.

Suzy: Okay. How much money are we talking about?

Mom: Never you mind that.

Suzy: But this is where it gets complicated, Mom. If we don't know how you are going to finance this grand plan, how do we know it can happen?

Mom: That is a fair question. I am going to give you a paper that tells you where all my important information is located. I will also tell you that Daddy and I have Long-Term Care Insurance, Social Security and good savings. If anything happens to me and Dad, we expect we will be able to pay for our care for the duration. But we want input on either home care or where we will go live if we haven't gotten that far yet. Neither of us has any intention of living with you kids.

Suzy: But, Mom.

Mom: No "buts," Suzy.

Suzy: Mom, Nana lived with us for a long time. It was the best years of my life to have her here. I'm not sure I want to give that up so readily. What if something happens to you or Dad and the other one is left behind. Dad will not do well by himself, Mom. You know that. We want you to move in with us. Jim and I have already talked about it.

Mom: See, Suzy? That's just what I mean. You and Jim have talked about it but not with us. I suppose the four of us should sit down and be as specific as we can. And we should include your brother. He needs to be a part of this, so there's no misunderstanding.

Suzy: Okay, yes let's do that soon.

Mom: No, Suzy, now. Let's make a plan now. Call your brother. And while we are at it, what's your plan if anything happens to you?

Suzy: Mom!

Mom: I'm not kidding. You know my friend Donna is taking care of her great-granddaughter right now. But she has no legal authority and it's a big mess. You aren't protected because you're young, Suzy. Get on the stick.

Suzy: Okay mom. Let's call Danny now before your soapbox gets so big I can't get out the door.

Mom: I get no respect.

What have we learned here?

Suzy is surprised that not only have her parents thought about the problems of health issues, but they have a plan, at least in theory. That plan does not coincide with Suzy's theoretical plan. Here's the road map for the conversation with your adult kids.

1. What is my/our plan as we get older for where we live?
   - Are we going to move now or in the future?
   - Where are we going to move?
   - If we are not going to move, can we stay where we are if we have health issues?
   - What do we expect from our adult children in terms of where we live?
   - Be as specific as possible about where you want to live. If you are considering an over-55, a step-down community, or something like that, which one? Where is it? Have you gone to visit it? Do you have friends there? The more specific you are, the more likely your decisions will be honored.

2. Do we have the finances for our plan?
   - Do we know how much assisted living, nursing homes and in-home care costs in our area?
   - Do we have Long-Term Care Insurance in place or is it a part of our life insurance, annuities or investments?
   - Do we expect the cost of care to be borne by our children in any way? This includes living with them, helping to pay for our living expenses, expecting them to do caregiving duties like driving, doctor's appointments, grocery shopping, household chores, etc. (*I have news for you. All of this costs time and money. If you expect your kids to chip in with cutting the grass, taking you to the doctor, etc. you are asking them for a financial investment, especially if it means they will give up working to help you. They are then giving up retirement funds, social security and a paycheck.*)

3. If we plan to be as self-sufficient as possible, have we done the preparation for that?
   - Legal Documents in order and updated:
     - Financial Power of Attorney
     - Health Care Power of Attorney/Proxy
     - Living Will
     - Will or Trusts as suggested by your lawyer
   - Finances in order and information about that available to your kids

4. Have we had a frank discussion with our adult children about the best possible scenario and about the worst-case scenario? A crisis has no boundaries. It can come for any one of us at any time. This preparation is a gift to your adult children, but it by no means can be perfect. It can only be as good as it can under the circumstances. The more you talk about it and everyone knows what you want, the easier it will be to make decisions under the duress of a crisis.

I know you are sensing a theme here: Get your legal documents and make sure they are updated. I want you to understand that there's a deeper reason for this than just 'get them.' These legal documents, especially your Powers of Attorney are the crux of every thing that must be done in a crisis. Your spouse will need them, your kids will need them, your doctors will need them, your financial advisors will need them, your insurance professional will need them, Medicare will need them, if you are a Veteran, the VA or Tricare or CHAMPVA will need them. And the list can go on and on. I am not the lawyer crying wolf here. I am the caregiver crying "Help!" because every member of your team, whether you assembled the team or your caregiving spouse, adult child, sister-in-law or dear friend assembled them, will demand this paperwork.

The ugly alternative is Guardianship. No one really wants that but if you fail to decide these things and put the paperwork in place you could very well end up like Britney Spears.

What happens if your adult children won't address this with you?

Dad: Tom, I want to talk about what's going to happen if I get sick.

Tom: Oh, Dad, don't be ridiculous.

Dad: Tom, I am 72 years old. Yes, I'm pretty fit and healthy, but you never know.

Tom: Well, then we will discuss it then.

Dad: Tom, if you don't want to talk about it, fine. But with or without you, I am going to make some plans so you may want to know how it involves you.

Tom: Dad, why do we have to do this now?

Dad: Okay. When would you like to do this? On Tuesday, when I am in the hospital, after a heart attack? Son, nobody knows what will happen. I've gotten up to 72 with no real issues, so this is as good a time as any.

Tom: Exactly. We've gotten this far, let's roll the dice.

Dad: See that's what you don't get. I'm not rolling the dice. I'm just letting you know how the dice will fall, depending on how much control I have in the moment.

Tom: Fine. Let's just do this and get it over with.

Dad: It's a good thing, son. Trust me. I don't have a lot of savings, but I do have some nursing home insurance that your dear, departed mother insisted I get long ago. So that will help. I have been looking at a community where some of my friends are on the waiting list and I signed up as well. It's called Arcadia and it's in the town close to you, so there's that. And I can stay there if I run out of money.

Tom: Whoa…what? Wait a minute! You're moving?

Dad: Not right away, but yes, I hope so. Tom, I'm lonely in this big, empty house. And I don't want to be a burden to you and Terri and the kids.

Tom: Dad…we were hoping you'd come live with us.

Dad: No, you weren't and even if you were, I want to be with my friends. Tom, there's so much to do there. Come with me. I'll show you!

Tom: Okay, Dad if that's what you want. Anything else I need to know?

Dad: Not really. I have all my paperwork together and, in a place, where you can find it. If we're lucky this is all just me moving to be with some friends.

Tom: Okay, Dad. I had no idea you were so unhappy.

Dad: I'm not unhappy, Tom. I'm just getting older and trying to be smart about what happens next.

Tom: Well…

Dad: See, that wasn't so bad. Now next week we will talk about what happens if I am in a permanent vegetative state!

Tom: DAD!!!

And yes, you should be having these discussions every week if necessary. However long it takes to get everyone on the same page. In the same breath, don't make this an epic tale. Decide what you want, figure out if or how you can do it and tell the important people in your life what you've decided.

CHAPTER SEVEN

A CONVERSATION WITH MY SIBLINGS

I have seven, count 'em, seven siblings, and I am still far from an expert in this field. Six of them would agree and the seventh would agree from heaven where I am quite certain she and my brother-in-law are laughing at me every single day.

Nonetheless, I will see if I can help you in any way with the rocky road, shark-infested waters of navigating care with siblings. There is no right answer, except that you will have a conversation eventually. If the first time is when the ambulance is taking Mom to the hospital, it probably won't go as well as if you had some of these conversations in advance.

Mom: Did you talk to your brother today?

Beth: No, do I need to talk to my brother today?

Mom: Well, he called me and I told him about the problems I was having with my eyes and he said he was going to talk to you about it.

Beth: Why? I mean what's he going to do from three thousand miles away?

74

Mom: Beth! What's that supposed to mean?

Beth: Sorry, that was uncalled for. I guess I'm just tired today.

Mom: Well, I should think so.

Beth: Mom, seriously, though, what do I need to discuss with Bill?

Mom: He just wants to know what's going on.

Beth: Well, didn't you tell him?

Mom: I told him you would tell him.

This seems innocent enough. Mom and Beth go to the doctor together because Mom needs an advocate and a second set of ears. If you are the child (with or without siblings) and Mom needs help you should definitely be doing this. Our health care system today is so fractured and so rife with ridiculous arbitrary rules about care that pretty much each and every one of us needs an advocate to go to bat for things like: a second opinion, a needed medical test, a needed non-generic drug, needed prescribed (so it gets paid for) durable medical equipment. I am all about having an advocate at your side with any doctor visit.

Here's the rub: Maybe Beth works full time. Maybe Beth has kids at home. Maybe Beth has her own health issues. Maybe Beth really is tired. Maybe Beth has three or four more siblings around who can pick up the slack. Maybe Beth is a control freak who needs to learn how to let go. Maybe Beth needs to share the wealth (and by that, I mean the burden).

Beth (texting her three siblings): Hey guys, we need to have a family meeting.

Bill: Okay, but I won't be home for two months.

Beth: We can Zoom.

Brigid: Zoom? OMG! I zoom every damn day for work. I am Zoomed out!

Brad: Fine. Send me the link.

Beth: Okay great. Brigid, you can come over to my house and we can Zoom together from here.

Brigid: Well, it depends on when you want to do this.

Beth: How about Sunday at ten AM?

Bill: That's seven AM here?!?

Beth: Oops, sorry forgot. How about noon, on Sunday?

Brad: Does it have to be a Sunday? I play golf.

Beth: OMG, you guys, this is about Mom and taking care of her. I need help. So, yeah. It has to be this Sunday.

Brigid: Brad, you can miss one day of golf.

Brad: Now you sound like my wife, Brig.

Bill: I gotta' go. Send me the link.

Beth: Fine. Sunday it is.

You can see that just getting a family meeting together with multiple siblings can be a challenge. But do it. You must, even if there are only two siblings. A while ago, my mom fell and broke her arm. At that time, I was caring for my brother-in-law with MS and my best friend who suffered a traumatic brain injury. I was tapped out. So, I did just this with my four sisters. I will even admit to you that I had a sexist meeting and did not include my two brothers. One does indeed live 3,000 miles away (and is a very good son) and the other lived two hours away at the time. The rest of us, all the sisters, were within a 20-minute driving range at most to be with my mom. I note this because as of this writing, although there are many, many good men out there who are caregivers, the brunt of caregiving continues to fall onto women's shoulders. This needs to be recognized and acknowledged because in the next chapter we discuss how this has an effect on our work, our savings and our retirement.

Our siblings need to come to understand how this is going to work and that it is an ever-changing process. Therefore, I recommend a family meeting. Here are some of the things you can address in the family meeting. Every family has its own quirks. You will be adding to or subtracting from to these ideas as you need to. And by the way, even though in my family meeting, my sister Tina became the designated control person, my mom still called me first. I would hang-up with Mom and call Tina to tell her what mom needed. So, there's that.

The most important thing here is that the family meeting is a tool that caregivers need to make use of, especially to avoid caregiver burnout.

QUESTIONS FOR A FAMILY MEETING:

1. Who is in charge of Mom's affairs? Or is it a shared duty situation?
   a. Do you have the requisite paperwork done (e.g. POA, HIPAA forms)?
   b. Are the right people on the requisite paperwork?

2. How the other siblings can help with defined duties:
   a. Bill paying
   b. Doctor Visits
   c. Grocery Shopping
   d. Hairdresser
   e. Church
   f. Home chores
   g. Car Maintenance
   h. Computer/Phone/TV help
   i. Meal Preparation
   j. Filling the Medicine Holder

3. What happens when it gets worse? (If Mom can't participate in the above and you now need to either get more help, consider a facility, or merely up your game as family caregivers.)
   a. Bathing
   b. Dressing
   c. Eating
   d. Ambulating
   e. Medicine Dosing and Administration

4. Family Caregiver Agreement
   a. Can we pay one or more of us to be the caregiver?
   b. Who gets paid?

      c. How much?

      d. Put the Caregiver Agreement in writing. (The end of this chapter has a Sample Caregiver's Agreement.)

5. Advanced Caregiving

      a. Who is in charge of the hiring and firing of paid caregivers in Mom's home?

      b. Who will research facilities for Adult Day Care?

      c. Who will research facilities for permanent placement?

6. If Mom is in a facility:

      a. Who is the point person for the facility?

      b. How will we structure visits to the facility to keep an eye on Mom's care?

      c. Who will speak to the administrator, facility physician, physical therapy, nursing staff? One sibling or shared duties?

From this list you can see that there are dozens of conversations that won't get resolved in one sunny, Sunday afternoon (or if Brad is lucky, it's pouring rain and his golf game got cancelled anyway). All of this is an important starting point to help Mom and protect that one sibling from the intense burden that goes along with being the primary caregiver.

And, yes. Someone needs to be in charge. Someone needs to be the decider. It seems like every family knows who that is. That's a good thing. But it doesn't mean you get to wash your hands and not help. The primary caregiver doesn't have the time or energy to do this delineation of duties by herself. That's the benefit of a family meeting. She will do a thousand things on her own first rather than ask you to go to the grocery store. She's going anyway, so she will get Mom her groceries, too. No. That's not how it should work if Brigid is in charge of grocery shopping. Beth needs to let go and the siblings need to help.

One thing I like to remind people of is this: If you, as a control-freak primary caregiver, do not allow siblings, friends, cousins, or anyone to help you, you are denying those wonderful helpers the opportunity to serve your loved one with grace and kindness. The giving of those gifts of service is priceless. If you, as the primary caregiver, refuse to allow others to help, you are taking from the helpers' time spent with their loved one, as well. Hmmm. What a thought. Maybe selfless and selfish are a bit too closely related. Whoever is related by blood or love, let them help!

This is a sample Caregiver's Agreement that is found on the Internet as a free download. There are several to choose from and many websites that will give you more complex versions, if you need it. This is important for Chapter 11 Conversations with a Caregiver as you may need a contract for a hired caregiver.

Additionally, and with an Elder Lawyer's assistance, there are many states that allow certain family members to be paid for caregiving services. This is an important part of the sibling conversation. If you go that route and rightfully pay a family member who is taking a financial hit by caregiving for your loved one, a caregiver contract is not only critical for family unity, it can play an important role in Medicaid Planning. A conversation with an Elder Lawyer may also be helpful in drawing up the terms of the contract.

Do not fall down the rabbit hole of taking advantage of a sister, daughter, cousin who is curtailing her work, or perhaps giving up an income altogether to care for a loved one. I don't care if her "husband makes a good living." She should be paid, if possible, and paid correctly. Social Security should be paid as well, or if you are going to 1099 (independent contractor) the caregiver, then the caregiver should be self-employed, pay her own Social Security out of her wages and take appropriate tax deductions for mileage and business expenses. This is where unpaid caregivers give too much without too much thought. This is where siblings need to come together to do the right thing by Mom and her caregiver.

The reason this is so important is because unpaid family caregivers are ending up destitute now and in their future. They are giving up retirement funds, work promotions, Social Security, even their own savings. We need to look at unpaid family caregivers differently. And it begins with us, those at home who are caregiving or finding our siblings caregiving and making a difference for the caregiver as well as the one cared for.

SAMPLE CAREGIVER AGREEMENT

CARE AGREEMENT

This agreement made this_____ day of _____, _____), by and between [*name of older adult*] (hereafter referred to as "_____"), and, _____, Caregiver (hereafter referred to as "Caregiver").

1. Purpose. The purpose of this agreement is to set forth the terms and conditions under which Caregiver will provide assistance with day to day living for _____ in his/her home in exchange for reasonable compensation.

2. Services to be performed by Caregiver. Caregiver shall furnish _____ with the services and incidentals specified herein, provided that _____ remains in his/her house and performs his or her obligations under this contract. In consideration of the mutual promises contain herein, the parties intent to be legally bound, agree as follows:

3. Nutrition.

a. Balanced meals- Caregiver hereby agrees to prepare three (3) nutritionally balanced meals per day when such assistance is requested. One such meal shall be served in the morning, one at mid-day, and one in the evening for _____.

b. Special Diet- Special diets will be provided only upon order of a licensed physician.

c. Additional Duties- Caregiver agrees to grocery shop for _____ with nutritious meals in mind. Following the preparation of meals, Caregiver shall assist with feeding, if necessary, and cleaning the kitchen which included washing dishes.

4. Cleaning. Caregiver agrees to provide cleaning services on a weekly basis as follows:

a. General cleaning

b. Make bed

c. Wash Laundry/ change sheets

d. Wash dishes

e. Empty waste containers

f. Sweep and mop all uncarpeted floor, stairs and hallways

g. Scrub floors

h. Disinfect all bathrooms

i. Replace bathroom supplies

j. Maintain bedroom in a neat and orderly condition

5. Housekeeping. _____ shall maintain the home in a clean and sanitary and orderly condition. Caregiver shall make available to _____ all supplies necessary for _____ to perform the usual housekeeping in order to maintain his or her accommodations. Caregiver shall perform all ordinary and heavy housekeeping as set forth in detail above.

6. Assistance outside the Home. Caregiver shall run daily errands for_____. These may include but are not limited to, picking up dry cleaning, grocery shopping, shopping for necessities and, if applicable, maintaining ___'s car.

7. Personal Care Needs. Caregiver shall observe _____'s physical and mental states on a regular basis, and shall make arrangements, as necessary, to meet health needs by arranging transportation to the physician of _____'s choice. Caregiver shall provide assistance to _____ in carrying out the instructions of physicians including storing, distributing and reminding _____ to take prescribing medications.

Caregiver shall also provide _____ with personal assistance with bathing, dressing, toileting, hair care, shaving, eating, care of clothing, personal shopping and incidental services, as needed.

8. Transportation. Caregiver shall assist with transportation needs by arranging for public transportation or help with specially provided elderly transportation.

9. Companionship and Entertainment. Caregiver shall provide companionship and support for _____.

10. Compensation. _____ shall pay Caregiver:

_____ Weekly _____ Monthly
On each ____ of the week/month $_____ per hour.

11. Governing Law, Entirety of Agreement and Severability. This agreement shall be governed by the laws of state of _____. It constitutes the entire agreement between the parties regarding its subject matter. If any provision in this contract is held by any court to be invalid, void or unenforceable, the remaining provisions shall nevertheless continue in full force and effect.

THIS IS A LEGALLY BINDING CONTRACT. EACH PARTY HAS READ THE ABOVE AGREEMENT BEFORE SIGNING IT. EACH PARTY UNDERSTANDS THE AGREEMENT THAT HE OR SHE IS MAKING.
We, _____ and Caregiver having read this agreement, agree to its terms and sign it as our free act on the _____ Day of _____,
_____.

_____

_____

[name of older adult] Caregiver
Witness

_____

_____

Signature Address

CARE AGREEMENT

This agreement made this____ day of _____, _____), by and between [*name of older adult*] (hereafter referred to as "_____"), and, _____, Caregiver (hereafter referred to as "Caregiver").

https://www.payingforseniorcare.com/caregiver-contract.pdf

CHAPTER EIGHT

A CONVERSATION WITH A DOCTOR...ANY DOCTOR

Inevitably, if you are getting older (and who isn't?) you will talk to a doctor. If you are a caregiver, you will be talking to a doctor for your caregivee. If you need a caregiver then they too, shall need to speak to a doctor on your behalf. Everyone's talking to a doctor these days! And btw, if you ARE a doctor, listen up, 'cause we're talking to you!

Margaret: Hello Dr. Z, nice to see you.

Dr Z: Nice to see you too, Margaret. Who is this you brought with you today?

Margaret: This is my daughter, Lisa.

Dr. Z: Hi, Lisa. Nice to meet you.

Lisa: Nice to meet you as well, Dr. Z. I have a lot of questions about my mom.

Dr. Z: Whoa, well, alright. Let's just see where we are at before we get to the questions, shall we?

Lisa: No, we shall not.

Margaret: Lisa!

Lisa: Sorry, Mom, but we are often hustled out of doctor's offices because they don't have the time to spend with you and we have a lot of questions about what is going on with your meds.

Dr. Z: I assure you, Lisa, I won't be hustling you out of here. But I'd like to get your mom's blood pressure, ask her a few questions about how she's been feeling and then we will get to your entire list, I promise.

Lisa: Okay, but that's the whole reason we are here. She has been feeling terrible and no one can figure out why.

Dr. Z: Let's see then. Everything looks pretty good. Tell me what's going on, Margaret.

Margaret: I'm tired. I'm listless. I get rashes for no reason and I have no appetite.

Lisa: It's even worse than that, Doctor. She's cranky, she's losing weight, she sleeps a lot, and she complains about nausea.

Dr. Z: Okay well, let's do some tests so we can see what's going on.

Lisa: I would like to file my mom's Health Care POA with your office as well. So that when I call and ask questions, they can read the records to me. I brought it with me so that your office can make a copy and put it in the record.

Dr. Z: Oh, well that would have to go to our Administrator.

Lisa: Yes, I know that. But I'm telling you this now in front of my mom, so that everyone is on the same page that I can get important information and ask questions even when my mom isn't available or doesn't want to, right?

Margaret: Lisa...I'm sorry, Dr. Z.

Dr.Z: It's fine, Margaret. She's only concerned about your health and well-being.

Lisa: Thank you, doctor. Please don't apologize, Mom. I'm not doing anything wrong. Also, I would like to have my mom fill out an updated HIPAA form so that everyone is on board with that as well.

Dr. Z: Well, I'm sure we can make that happen with the Administrator.

Lisa: Can we do that today, since we are both here?

Dr.Z: I don't know, but you can ask at the desk.

Lisa: Dr. Z. My mom adores you. She is very happy with the care she gets here at your office...

Dr. Z: Thank you, Lisa...

Lisa: However...that being said, it's really important that we get things squared away today, as I don't live here and need to get as much done as possible to help my mom while I'm here. I hope you can help me with your staff if I run into any problems.

Margaret: Lisa....

Dr. Z: It's okay, Margaret, really, I understand your daughter's concern.

And yes, she isn't doing anything wrong. The fact that Lisa is in the doctor's office speaks volumes. It is critically important for Lisa, and all caregivers, to establish that they are not just transportation. Caregivers are there to assist, and if necessary, speak for their loved one. Having a frank discussion with your loved one's doctor should sound like this and everyone should be fine with it, especially you and the physician.

One of the most important factors here is that you are making certain that the physician has the Power of Attorney so that you, the caregiver, can talk to the doctor or his staff in the future.

What about specialists? What about Emergency Room doctors? What about a pharmacist, a physical therapist, a chiropractor? First, if possible, they need that document of authority, the POA. If not possible, you can always tell them you have such a document and will assure that they get it posthaste (ye olde English for ASAP). You can keep a copy on your phone in fact. I don't worry so much about sharing abundantly a Healthcare POA as it is not filled with personal information that would cause a problem if found by a stranger. AND because the medical field, in a pinch, is willing to wait for the document if you claim to have it!

Let's imagine a conversation with a medical provider where you don't have such a document.

Dr. John: Hello, Larry. How are you feeling today?

Larry: Not so great.

Dr. John: Yes, your tests came back pretty dismal. As we discussed last time, you will need to start the new medication and start making plans for some changes in your life.

Larry: Yes, I realize that. I want you to be able to speak to my sister whenever I need help.

Dr. John: You can put that in your chart.

Larry: I already did, and some of the staff gave her a hard time. They said she wasn't my wife. I don't have a wife.

Dr. John: I'll make a note of that and tell them to check the chart.

Larry: Is that all I need to do?

Dr. John: As long as you put in your sister as the point of contact, we should be okay.

Larry: Great.

NO, NO, THIS IS NOT GREAT. Do not depend on the medical profession to give you advice that is not medical. It will come to bite you in the arse if you don't have the right Healthcare Power of Attorney as well as HIPAA forms. Some consider those forms redundant and I agree. But I really don't want to be in the middle of an Emergency Room screaming: "My POA is just as good as a HIPAA!"

It may take some time before they discover you don't have the appropriate paper work. Like I said, the medical community is pretty forgiving and will often talk to relatives, especially in a crisis, for some time before they demand the legal paperwork that allows it. This is especially true with spouses. But a long time is not forever, and God forbid, you get to a phase with someone who suffers from a chronic illness like ALS, MS, Alzheimer's and you went along with just being heard because you were a spouse, or a family caregiver. And then your loved one is truly unable to communicate and you don't have the requisite legal documents to give you the necessary authority to make important decisions.

Now that you've had the document conversation what else do you need to discuss with your physician or the physician of a loved one?

Where else can conversations with physicians be treacherous?

1. When they don't address your actual health problem
2. When they don't refer you to an expert
3. When you don't have the courage to ask for a second opinion
4. When they don't let you take notes
5. When they don't spend enough time with you
6. When they won't take your paperwork and put it on file
7. When they ask for the wrong paperwork i.e., a living will
8. When they assume your loved one has dementia because they have a UTI
9. When they don't know your loved one so they make assumptions based on age, color, sex, weight, socioeconomic factors...i.e., their prejudice is showing
10. When they don't work with therapists, chiropractors, mental health professionals, social workers, lawyers, other family members

11. When their arrogance prevents them from seeing and hearing you i.e., they don't listen

OH, THOSE OUCHY DOCTOR CONVERSATIONS!

As I am writing this book, caregivers of all kinds give me glorious suggestions about conversations that need to be had. Let's examine a few here with doctors, both from the patient perspective, the caregiver perspective and the physician perspective

1. The Stop Driving Conversation

   Dad: Okay, Doc, thanks for everything. We will see you next year.

   George: Not so fast, Dad. Doctor, I'd like to talk about Dad's driving.

   Dad: What? We aren't going to bother the doctor with that.

   George: Yes, yes, we are.

   Doctor: Well, my goodness, are you still driving, Tom?

   Dad: Yeah, to the store, to get my hair cut, to the card game.

   George: He's had a few incidents, shall we say.

   Doctor: What kind of "incidents?"

   Dad: Oh, it's nothing. Just a few wrong turns.

George: Yes, down a one-way street, left on a red light. It's not safe.

Doctor: Tom...

Dad: I'm fine, Doc. I'll be more careful.

George: You've said that before, Dad. It's not safe for you or for other people. What if there's a baby in somebody's car that you hit?

Doctor: Tom...you need to stop.

George: Doctor, you need to take his keys. We've talked about this and he doesn't commit.

Doctor: Well, I'm sure Tom understands. Don't you, Tom?

Dad: Sure, Doc.

George: Okay look guys. We need an agreement here and now, before someone, either my dad, or some innocent bystander, gets hurt. Doc, I need you to take Dad's keys and do whatever you do with the state to make sure he can't drive.

Doctor: That seems harsh, George.

George: Really? How harsh will it seem when my dad is in an accident at his age.   Even if he agrees here, he will forget that he agreed. He will do what he pleases.

Doctor: Tom, it's time to stop.

Dad: How am I supposed to get anywhere?

George: That is a good question, Dad. And I promise you, I have set up an Uber and Lyft account for you. You call me or them and we will make sure you get where you need to go or want to be.

Doctor: See, Tom. It will work out.

You can have this conversation without a doctor, but it is often better to have another expert in the room, especially if your loved one has health conditions that are not conducive to driving. It is usually easier to have this "no more driving" conversation when you have other solutions in place. And don't use, 'you can call me anytime' as a solution. You know you are busy, even if you live with your loved one that you are caring for. We ARE fortunate to live in the time of Uber and Lyft! You have to have solutions for the person whose liberty you are curtailing. There is often Senior Transport offered by Aging and Adult Services in your town. There may be taxi service as well as Uber and Lyft. If you are able to hire a driver for your dad who is at his beck and call, fantastic. But taking away driving privileges without recognizing that your loved one needs to and wants to get places is cruel. Have a plan, which is what this entire book is about, making plans.

Sometimes taking the keys, selling the car, or just disabling it with a flat tire, a removed part (I have no clue about cars so this is where I could say carburetor, alternator, or radiator hose and not know if that even exists in your car or would make a difference…so I just say parts, and you can figure it out!) will solve the first part of the problem. But don't assume your loved one will find a resolution. I know you are the caregiver and you have enough to do. You are saving lives here, theirs, yours and maybe someone you will never meet. Do the homework.

Back to the doctor.

You may get help here and you may not. In some states, doctors are technically legally required to notify the Department of Transportation if someone is medically unfit to drive. Then the Department will likely pull the driver's license, revoking all driving privileges.

CAVEAT: Here's something you should know. You *need a photo ID in this world.* A driver's license, if you have one, is the easiest thing to use for photo ID. Your loved one may have a passport, which is also great and good for 10 years. If you do have a driver's license pulled by the Department, you usually can get an ID card, but what if you can't get your loved one out to get that card? Having a driver's license revoked and no additional photo ID can be problematic.

This happened to me.

I was the primary caregiver for my brother-in-law, Larry. Larry had Multiple Sclerosis and it was the worst possible kind. It was progressive and unrelenting. In short order, Larry had to use his wheelchair every day, all day. He also needed hired caregivers for dressing, meds and preparing for bed. All of this required a Hoyer Lift to get Larry in and out of bed, since lifting him became impossible. Transporting Larry to doctor's appointments, physical therapy or any other place was a gargantuan task because he gave up driving long before he was in a facility, and eventually, since I could not lift him, even with help from the other brawny men in my life to get him into my car, I needed paid transportation.

What do you do? You fight with insurance for transportation. Sometimes you win, most times you lose. But in the meantime, he surely did not need a driver's license. Yet Medicare created a requirement that they would not allow patients to be seen by any medical providers without the patient first providing photo ID! I had managed to get Larry to the photo ID place in my own car four years earlier, but now his license was expiring. It had become impossible to Larry to the photo license center on my own. I was in a panic because his family doctor's staff cautioned me that his license was expiring and I would need a new one. This is how it went:

Receptionist: You will need to make sure Larry's ID is current next time you come.

Me: How do you propose I do that?

Receptionist: He needs to get a new driver's license.

Me: First, he has been coming here for *twenty years.* It's not like you don't know him from his expired license and photo. Second, even if *you* don't know him, the doctor knows him because he has been his patient *for twenty years.* Third, I can get him ambulance transport here to see a doctor, which we still have to pay for, but they will not transport Larry to a non-medical place for a paltry photo ID. So, I ask you again, how do you propose I do that?

Receptionist: (mumble, mumble, mumble)

Me: Yes, I do have to be a witch about it. That is what you said, right? Because I don't actually know how to comply with these ridiculous rules. Let me ask you something? If Larry were in a nursing home and not independent living, where the doctor goes to see the patients who haven't left that nursing home for months or years, do those patients have to have a current ID?

Receptionist: I don't know. Probably not.

Me: Fine. Then we will cross this bridge next time. I will do my best, but I am making no guarantees and the medical profession needs to stand up for its patients as well. Have a nice day.

Okay, fine. I wasn't well-liked there every time I went. If you have been or are a caregiver you know that sometimes your ire gets the best of you and may be misplaced, or may be placed quite well, thank you very much. I'm still debating many years later if I should have been less "witchy." Ummm. No.

If you are lucky enough, as I was, to befriend a rogue ambulance driver who I had met many times in my transportation journey with Larry, you may need to find another way. That good man took me to the Driver's License photo place on the way to a doctor's appointment. Creativity in caregiving is a must!

Friends, my point here is, disable the car, take the license, take the car, get the doctor on board, but maybe do not "pull" the license if you have no passport or other way to get a current ID. Then keep your loved one's license in your wallet.

MY PET PEEVE

R-E-S-P-E-C-T.

I started taking my Nana to the doctor when I was a teenager. My Nana died when I was thirty-eight years old. I had plenty of experience with taking a loved one to see a physician. Over time I noticed that Nana went from being, "Mrs. Repko," to "Margaret." And the doctors, of course, got younger and younger. None of which mattered...I mean their youth. If they got through medical school and were here in this office, I'm pretty good with that. But my Nana is a woman of substance, wisdom and grace. Age has earned a place for respect and I am loathe to let it go. In my first book, *Showering with Nana: Confessions of a Serial (killer)Caregiver,* I recount a tale where a physician made an emergency house call to help my ailing Nana. This doctor had never met my Nana. I was supremely grateful that he came to our home and quite surprised as house calls were already a thing of the past. But it grated on my nerves how he called my Nana by her given name the entire time, without asking permission.

I know it's silly, even ridiculous. But if you live into your seventh, eighth, or ninth decade, even if you are not the nicest person, you deserve a bit of respect in the doctor's office. Just ask if I can use your first name. Oh, and if you don't know how to pronounce or spell my name ask that, too. My mom's name is Mary Ann. *Not Mary.* Mary Ann. And she really gets frosted when doctors, nurses, therapists or anyone else calls her Mary, which she should. Her name is Mary Ann, not Mary. But often my mom is too nice to say anything, except to me when we get back out to the car. Before I end up taking all of her wrath, I nip it in the bud in the office...'cause you know, I'm the "witchy" one!

CHAPTER NINE

A CONVERSATION WITH MY LAWYER—ANY LAWYER

You really must speak to a lawyer at least once in your life to get this important paperwork in order. I hesitate to repeat here if you are breezing through this book. But if you only picked it up to read this Chapter then I will save you the horror of having to page through and say, "What darn documents is she talking about?" For the rest of you intrepid souls just wash over the next few paragraphs until you get to the Q & A for you and the lawyer.

THE DOCUMENTS:

If you are starting this book here, here is a quick summary of "the documents." They are the true FINAL FOUR! You will need them now, if you get sick, or if you plan or don't plan on dying.

1. Durable Financial Power of Attorney
2. Health Care Power of Attorney or Health Care Proxy
3. Living Will or Advanced Directive
4. Will

Each of these requires a detailed conversation with your lawyer or a lawyer. I prefer you speak to an Elder Lawyer because each state of these United States has their own quirks about how to make these documents work for you and your situation. Here's an idea, followed by some questions you should immediately be putting out there.

First, let's talk about money. The number one objection to going to see a lawyer is, "I can't afford it." The number one lie is, "I can't afford it." Most of you reading this book can afford it. You don't want to pay for it. You think it is either a waste of money, unnecessary, or too expensive for the pieces of paper you will be taking home with you.

How else can I say this: You're wrong. If you have picked up or been given a book to read about how to prepare for aging, caregiving, and retirement, you are looking at how to save or protect assets...spelled m-o-n-e-y. This means you have some money and you don't want to share it, at least not with some lawyer you never met. I get it. Let me reassure you, this lawyer you never met wants to help you save money too, and heartache, and stress and dyspepsia. Our job as Elder Lawyers is to create a safe environment for the future, as much as we can, so that if and when a crisis of health or wealth occurs you have legal protections in place to ease the road to navigate those crises.

How do you know if you are getting ripped off or not? Start with the telephone. Call lawyers in your area who advertise as Elder Lawyers and ask them how much it costs to have a consultation or create the Final Four documents (Note: I call them the Final Four, which I think is devilishly creative but they might not know what you mean by that so you have to say the names of the documents!) They may have a consultation fee or not. They may not wish to quote a price because it depends on your situation, ask for a ball park. If they won't play with you, move on. You have every right to know how much you will be spending.

Given their experience and expertise you will pay a few hundred to a few thousand dollars. The price range has to do with how much you have in assets. Is your asset life complex? Do you have a bunch of real estate, stock accounts, IRAs, 401ks? Do you and your spouse have a blended family? Do you have people you hate and want to make sure they get absolutely nothing? Do you have a favorite actual Final Four team that you want to leave a legacy to? Do you just have a dog and a favorite chair and someone you love you hope will take care of you? See? They can't possibly know that in a five minute 'how much does it cost?' conversation. But they can tell you a range of fees. Ask for that if that is your hang-up.

I am here to tell you that cost is not your biggest objection. You can NOT afford to be without these documents. You and your partner can lose precious assets to nursing homes, taxes and even those people you don't like if you don't do the paperwork. And I know you all know about Aretha Franklin, Larry King, Prince and tons of other celebrities who died without their paperwork. I'm actually less concerned about your death than I am about your sickness. Do you want to be sick with a court deciding who makes important decisions for you? Do you want to be chronically ill and all your assets go to your care leaving your significant other destitute? Do you really want to die and have your family fighting over what you left behind rather than celebrating your precious life? To be fair, my great-aunt who worked for a lawyer for 40 years wanted exactly that. She purposely left no will so that everyone would fight over her useless, cumbersome, elephantine antiques that crowded and shrouded her apartment for some seventy years. If that is your goal, then yes, stay home.

But most of you are nice people, with nice families. You have worked hard and you want to have a say in where your money goes in sickness and in death. So here is how you talk to a lawyer.

Sally: Hi Ms. Lawrence. It's nice to meet you.

Lawyer: Hi, Sally. So nice to meet you and your husband, John. Tell me what I can do for you today?

John: We need to update our wills and whatever else we need.

Lawyer: Okay, great. You filled out some preliminary information so I think we can talk about your situation.

Here is where you will discuss the things that are important to you. Each family is so different that this could go on for chapters in many ways. We will do some general things here so that YOU know what should be asked and what you should ask the lawyer. Then I will give you a list of items that should also be discussed. If those items are important to you, make sure you are talking about them with your lawyer.

Lawyer: Let's talk about the Powers of Attorney first. I see that you don't have those documents so we need to talk about why they are important and the job it entails. The Durable Financial Power of Attorney is a document that allows someone to act as if they are you in any capacity, if you become incapacitated. Just because you have each other, doesn't mean your spouse is legally allowed to act as if they are you. That's an important distinction that many spouses don't understand.

John: Hmmm. Like I can't sign her name to things?

Lawyer: Exactly. Not now or ever without this document.

John: Uh oh.

Lawyer: Clearly, we need to fix this now. I also want you to understand that this becomes critically important if either one of you is so sick you can't make decisions or sign documents. And since I see that you have several accounts listed as IRA's and 401ks, you need to know that without this Durable Financial POA you wouldn't have access to those funds in the other spouse's name.

Sally: Wait a minute. Wait. A. Minute. You mean, if John has a stroke or even just an accident, I can't get any money out of his IRA?

Lawyer: That is exactly what I mean.

Sally: But I'm his wife. We *live on that money?!*

Lawyer: The good news is you're here and we are going to fix it.

Sally: That could have been a nightmare. I mean, that would be devastating for me. How would I live? How would I pay the bills?

Lawyer: Exactly. And even more disastrous is that if it is a permanent disability for John and he really can't handle his affairs, you would ultimately have to seek guardianship.

John: Oh no, no we've seen those movies and documentaries about guardianship. I do not want that to happen.

Lawyer: Great, then we are all on the same page. Now let's talk about who will be in charge if both of you *are* incapacitated?

Sally and John: WHAT?!

Lawyer: Don't panic. I just want to discuss picking a person of your choice as an alternate POA in case you need it. It's like putting in an insurance policy right in the document. We just need you to decide who will be in charge of your financial affairs or your health care.

If your lawyer does not ask you about an Alternate POA you need to bring it up before you leave the office. Or maybe just leave the office since the lawyer is not addressing your needs. Seriously, just ask the question.

Lawyer: Now that we have chosen your Alternate and discussed some of the other details, let's talk about your wills. It looks like the last time you updated these your children were quite young.

John: Yes, it's time now that we are grandparents.

Lawyer: Great. Let's talk about where you want your assets to go when you pass away.

Sally: We want everything to go to our kids evenly.

Lawyer: We can do that. What if something happens to one of your children and they die before you?

John: Oh, we hadn't thought of that.

Lawyer: Do you want their share to go to their spouse or your grandchildren?

John: I'd like their spouses to get something. They married good kids.

Sally: John, their spouses will be fine. I want our assets to go to our grandkids for college.

Lawyer: To tell you the truth, we can do both. You don't have to have identical wills. If your child predeceases you, you can choose different options. This is your decision and it can truly be what you want as your legacy.

I just wanted you to know that spouses don't have to have identical wills!

John: That's fine with me.

Sally: Me, too. I want mine to just go to the grandkids.

John: And I want mine thirty per cent to the spouse and seventy percent to the grandkids.

Lawyer: I can do that. No problem. Now you need to pick a Trustee. Someone who will be in charge of the grandkids money if they are still minors when you die.

Sally: This is so complicated! I had no idea we would need to make so many decisions.

Lawyer: Yes, I understand. We want to get it right. That is why we have you complete all that paperwork before you get here, so we don't need to use even more of your time while discussing these important decisions.

That's the easy scenario. It could go so many ways. I'm hoping you will find that this is truly an important task you need to complete for yourself or your older (or younger!) loved ones. This is not for the faint of heart. You've got to get it done. And let me reiterate that when my children went to college, I made them do this process as well, for two reasons. One, I did not want any college administrator or hospital ER doctor telling me they wouldn't give me information on my child because she was an adult at age 18 and hadn't given them permission to consult with me. And two, I wanted my children to understand at a young age how important this process is and how it should be revisited at the important stages in your life.

One more topic to cover before we get to the list of questions for your lawyer. What is the difference between an Elder Lawyer and an Estate Lawyer? I present an entire webinar on this topic, so here's the skinny.

It's the difference between life and death.

Yes. An Elder Lawyer is trained to assist you with the issues during life. Issues surrounding aging and retirement. For example, nursing homes, Medicare, Medicaid (which sound alike but are two completely different things), long-term care plans, legal issues around dementia, caregiving, Social Security, etc.

The real thrust of an Elder Lawyer's work is: *How do I prepare for getting sick, old and maybe incapacitated?* It has nothing to do with being dead. Just yesterday, a friend of mine told me he and his wife didn't need to review his old paperwork because he had qualified accounts (meaning IRA, 401k or 403b, or investments along those lines) and they were beneficiary designated so no problem. He knew who would get his money.

That's if you die. If you're dead, your beneficiaries will *inherit* (we all know this is a word used for dead people) your qualified account. But if you are alive and sick, how does your spouse, adult child or person you've chosen to be in charge get *access* to your money in that qualified account? We've discussed this before but you can only benefit from a reminder and if you didn't read that chapter, it's important here as well.

The answer is, they don't without a Power of Attorney. Not even your spouse. Being a spouse in this instance gives you no special powers or privilege. If you don't have a POA that gives your spouse access to your investments that are owned solely by you, no bank or financial institution is going to give you any of that money. And don't be talking to this book saying, "well, all my accounts are joint, so I have no problem there!" You know the answer to that from previous chapters. If you are only reading this chapter, note that if you own one IRA, 401k, 403b or any qualified account, they are individually owned by law. They cannot be joint accounts, *ever*. And so, we circle back to you'd better have a POA in place if you want your spouse to have access to your funds in the case of illness, disability or incapacity. If you don't give them that POA for access and they need that money, and they can't wait until you die to inherit it, you will need a court to appoint a Guardian.

Often people think: I can wait for my spouse's big, fat 401k because we have other assets I can live on! Remember, your spouse is in a nursing home in this scenario. The nursing home is expecting you to pay them somewhere in the neighborhood of $8,000 to $12,000 a month for your sick spouse's care. Where are you going to get that money? This is in the next chapter when we talk to your financial advisor. For now, we are talking about the legal means to get that money. How and why you need access in case one of you gets ill. And that's why you need to talk to a lawyer before it happens.

Beneficiaries are important. And we will discuss the need for checking that on a regular basis. But do not, do not, do not confuse beneficiary designations with powers of attorney. Wills and beneficiaries are for dead people. Powers of Attorney are for live people who are sick or incapacitated and cannot handle their own affairs.

This bears repeating:

Wills and beneficiaries are for dead people. Powers of Attorney are for live people who are sick or incapacitated and cannot handle their own affairs.

This leads us to the difference between an Elder Lawyer and an Estate Lawyer. Estate Lawyers have probably been around since the Magna Carta (that's 1215 A.D. in case you didn't want to look it up). These fine attorneys deal with wills, trusts, estates and what happens to your stuff when you die. It is a gravely (see what I did there?) important job. Most Elder Lawyers, except for the young whippersnappers today, were probably Estate Lawyers first. That is because Elder Law is a fairly new area of the law that began taking shape around the 1980's.

Elder Law, as previously mentioned, is concerned with Powers of Attorney for financial issues, Health Care Powers of Attorney, Medicaid issues, especially as it applies to paying for that enormously expensive nursing home bill, Social Security, Medicare, and all the problems that can arise legally around aging and caregiving.

The two areas of law do overlap constantly, which is why both types of lawyers do advertise that they draft Wills, Trusts, Powers of Attorney, Living Wills and Advanced Directives. As the consumer, you need to ensure that the lawyer you choose is up-to-date in the state you live in about the laws around Elder Law. Estate Law hasn't changed much since King John and the Magna Carta, except for those pesky tax issues which keep changing all the time. Do not discount the importance of Estate planning.

Elder Law is changing all the time and the documents and the financial decisions that go into an Elder Law plan or a long-term care plan, or a crisis plan because Dad just had a stroke and no one knows what to do about it, are ever evolving.

So here are the questions you need to ask your lawyer:

1. Are you an Elder Lawyer or an Estate Lawyer? Is there a difference?
   a. Possible answers: I am both, I am an Estate Lawyer, have been for 30 years.
   b. RED FLAG: There is no difference.

2. How long have you been an Estate Lawyer and how long have you been doing Elder Law?
   a. Possible Answers: I specialize in Elder Law/or only Estate Law for X years
   b. RED FLAG: I do General Practice so this is a part of everything I do.

3. Do you have specific Gifting Language in your Powers of Attorney that protects my spouse? How do you feel about Gifting and adult children?
   a. Possible Answers: Gifting is a very important part of Powers of Attorney; There are several ways to look at Gifting, so I am glad you asked that question
   b. RED FLAG: We have standard gifting language that the state provides. Spouses don't need to worry about gifting.
4. Can you explain the Five Year Look Back issue in Gifting?
5. If you are recommending a trust of any kind, is it revocable or non-revocable? What is the difference?
6. How do you fund the trust?

7. Why are we doing a trust as opposed to a will?
   a. How much IS probate in my state?
   b. How are my assets protected in case of a nursing home issue with a trust as opposed to a will?
   c. Who will put my assets into the trust? How does that work?
   d. If it is an Irrevocable Trust, is there any concern about how my spouse and I would get assets in any other emergency?
8. How many trusts have you done? Can I speak to any of your clients about their satisfaction with that kind of a decision?
9. Do you check beneficiary designations of documents outside of your documents to see if everything is on the same page?
10. Will you have a conversation with me and my financial advisor to make certain we are all on the same page as to my long-term care, aging, retirement and legacy issues?

These ten questions are designed to help you distinguish several things:
   1. Is this person really an Estate Lawyer and NOT an Elder Lawyer?
   2. Is this person not an Elder Lawyer or an Estate Lawyer?
   3. Is this person willing to work with me and my financial advisor to ensure my long-term care plan and estate plan are all on the same page?

You will be able to figure this out, not by getting a law degree but by knowing some of the answers in a general way. Remember, you are *hiring* this person. Just as you are hiring or have hired a financial planner. You are interviewing this person for a job, for which you will be paying them. There is always benefit in asking your friends if they have an Elder Lawyer and if they are happy with them. Recommendations are always a good idea. But that does not mean you should not do your due diligence. I'm less concerned about how much it costs to get the paperwork done than I am concerned about how much it may cost you if you get it done improperly.

This story just came across my email. A client of a fellow Elder Lawyer came in to ask for assistance in applying for his wife to receive some much-needed Medicaid At-Home Care services. He had gone to the Elder Lawyer previously and got certain things taken care of, but in the interim, the client decided that his Estate Lawyer could move some assets around into an irrevocable trust (note the term *irrevocable* because it really does mean that...cannot be revoked). This Estate Lawyer completely ruined the Medicaid plan. By taking that action, the Estate Lawyer and client created a period of ineligibility for the wife. In other words, the seriously-ill wife *was* receiving Medicaid. But the lawyer who wasn't aware of that plan made some grievous mistakes, taking the wife off of Medicaid. Now, the healthy husband who had assets of his own that were protected so that husband could live his life, and maybe even leave a legacy of some kind to his kids was now in jeopardy of losing much of his money.

This is exasperating for Elder Lawyers, not a one of us, needs to be in competition with each other. There is no reason Estate and Elder Lawyers can't work together. There is really no reason why lawyers and financial advisors, accountants and insurance professionals can't work together. But when we all pretend we are experts in everything, you, our clients suffer. That's why you need to ask the important questions. Be not afraid. Ask the questions. Have the real conversations here. That's kind of the point of reading this book.

CHAPTER TEN

A CONVERSATION WITH A FINANCIAL ADVISOR

Some of you will not have a financial advisor, and that's fine. You may be well in charge of your finances and have decided to take care of this part of your life on your own. You may be quite financially savvy and have created a nice nest egg for yourself. Or, in the alternative, you think that your savings are not enough to warrant financial advice. I am a big fan of getting expert information wherever and whenever I can. And yes, I know Google has all kinds of cool stuff you can look up, but it does not replace expertise, it only adds to it. Google, yes. Stop there, no. Even if you have never been to a financial advisor, I would like to suggest that you might benefit from one visit with someone. Someone you've researched (yeah, I know 'researched' means Googled), someone who was recommended by a trusted friend or other professional like your accountant or lawyer. Just one meeting, if necessary, to see if either of you can shed any light on how to implement a plan if you and/or your spouse/partner becomes ill.

I will be honest it can be daunting. Tread lightly and feel secure that you are allowed to get information without investing anything. I sincerely hope you can find a financial advisor who can have a conversation with you and who provides you with enough information for you to make a decision as to whether you need them as an additional expert on your team. Your lawyer, accountant and insurance professional may be enough for you. That being said, if you do have a financial advisor, you should be having the long-term care conversation. If you haven't had it, shame on somebody. Shame on them, if they haven't brought it up. Shame on you if you said, "I don't want to talk about it." More than one professional has told me that should be the title of this book. "I don't want to talk about it!" But as you can see, we took a more proactive approach.

Cost of care for in-home care, personal care, assisted living and skilled nursing facilities runs on average anywhere between $4,000 to $12,000 per month. Yes, per month. And, no Medicare doesn't pay for that. We are talking about how much it costs to be cared for if you or your spouse, partner, or loved one becomes ill. Even if you can afford some of that, how are you going to use your assets to pay for it? That's why you need to talk to a financial advisor.

The reason I believe these are precarious conversations is that there are plenty of financial advisors who don't make long-term care a part of their plan. They believe that is either your insurance guy's problem, or if you really wanted it you would ask. Many financial advisors are hell-bent on making you money. Yay! But this conversation about what happens when I can't be making money but need money, and yet, I'm not dead, should be perhaps the first conversation you have with a financial advisor.

So how does it go? First, be open to this conversation if your financial advisor brings it up. Be completely open. And this book will give you the questions to ask. Next, if they haven't brought it up yet, and if you have been with this financial advisor for years…now is the time. You bring it up. Let's get this party started! It will be fun! I know you are skeptical.

Joanne: Hello, Joe. I want to discuss some long-term care questions I have with you.

Joe: That's great. Will Steve be joining us?

Joanne: Eventually, I wanted to ask a few things first, and then both of us can come in and dive into it. Is that okay?

Joe: Um, sure. I guess so.

Joanne: Great. I was wondering why we never discussed long-term care.

Joe: Well, Joanne, to be honest with you, I've approached this with Steve and he didn't want to talk about it. He said he wasn't going to any nursing home and he would just die.

Joanne: That does not surprise me at all. But, Joe, I can't ever remember you bringing this up when we were in your office together.

Joe: You may be right about that Joanne. But since I knew Steve wasn't on board, I guess I thought, "what's the point?" Especially since the bulk of your assets are in Steve's 401k.

Joanne: What does that mean?

Joe: Well, if the money to fund any kind of long-term care product has to come from somewhere, I just assumed it would have to come from Steve's money and Steve would not approve that.

Joanne: Excuse me? Did you say Steve's money?

Joe (realizes his mistake and tries to make it better): I mean, it's an IRA, so it's legally only in one name, Steve's name, so for legal purposes it's Steve's money, but I didn't mean that it wasn't family money.

Joanne: Well, by not including me in that conversation or even just that 'thought' you had, it's not family money, means you didn't think it was a conversation I should be included in.

Joe: You're right. I apologize. Sounds like we all need to have a meeting.

Okay, I know that sounds snarky. My financial advisor friends are either laughing or want to have words with me. Remember, this is about YOU. What happens to you, what happens to your money, what happens if you need help? I could write the same conversation about lawyers who don't refer clients to Elder Lawyers when the crisis is actually happening. I will take the heat for you, because it is critical to do the best we can now, before it's too late.

Joe: Thanks for coming in, Joanne and Steve.

Steve: I know why we are here and I don't wanna' talk about it.

Joanne: Well, I do and if you just want to listen instead of talk, that might be a good idea.

Steve: Hmph.

Joanne: So, Joe, what happens if Steve has a massive stroke tomorrow? Where does our money go? Am I protected? Or, as I'm reading up on this, is all "Steve's money," meaning his IRA, going to the nursing home and I'm up the creek?

Joe: I've done some homework on this and it's a bit complicated, but you are right that there are challenges when the bulk of your investments are in an IRA.

Steve: What does that mean?

Joe: Well, as Joanne pointed out before this meeting, your family money is in your house, your stock accounts, Joanne's small IRA and then the large majority of it is in Steve's IRA. So, Joanne's question is very important because if something happens to you, Steve, Joanne needs to have some things in place to figure out how the money works.

Steve: Well, what does that mean?

Joe: As far as I can tell, it means that if you stroke out tomorrow, Joanne may not have access to your IRA and a nursing home may believe that all that money should go to them.

Steve: What? Wait, what? She's my wife. She should be able to get to that money.

Joe: Okay, let's not get ahead of ourselves. That is obviously worst-case scenario. But after talking to an Elder Lawyer and our legal department the first thing Joanne would need is legal access to all your accounts.

Steve: But she's my wife. And I'm her husband.

Joe: Yeah, that's not enough.

Steve: What does that mean?

Joe: It means that both of you need written documents to let the other one have access to your money. Without a Financial Power of Attorney our legal department would not let you have access to each other's IRA for any reason. It would take a court order.

Steve: Wow. I had no idea.

Joanne: I did. I read it somewhere. But that still doesn't answer how we would pay for long-term care.

Steve: I told you. I'm just going to die. Just take me out and finish me off.

Joanne: Steve, it doesn't work that way. Plus, I'm not going to jail for anyone, so you can forget the finishing you off part.

Joe: Steve, Joanne has a point. It's just something to consider. Because even if one of you is sick only temporarily, you need a few things. You need Powers of Attorney and you need to know the cost of care, whether it's in your house, in a facility, whether it's temporary or permanent.

Steve: I get the Power of Attorney, even though I'm not sure how that works. But why do I need to know the cost of something I won't use. I'll just pay for it, if I need it.

Joanne: Ugh. Joe, please help.

Joe: Steve, I get what you're saying. And knowing the cost of care doesn't actually cost you anything.

Steve: Well, I guess that's true.

Joe: Great. The cost of care is $12,000 a month.

Steve, Joanne: WHAT?

Joe: I'd like to say 'just-kidding' but no, I'm not. Look obviously, there's all kinds of options but this is the reality. So, let's talk about it at length

Steve: Okay, I guess we should do this now.

Joanne: Good. Let's talk about it.

Joe: We need to get your paperwork in order and that requires an Elder Lawyer. Do you have a lawyer?

Steve: Only the guy who helped us with our house 30 years ago.

Joanne: No, Joe, we don't have a lawyer.

Joe: Okay, I can recommend one. Now we can work on putting a plan together.

This is the dream. That you and your financial advisor come to a place where you both understand the importance of this conversation. If you're lucky, your financial advisor starts the conversation...and finishes it. When I say finishes it, I mean that after much consideration, after understanding the cost, your personal situation, and what you truly want in case of a long-term care situation, you create a legally and financially sound plan that you can live with, until you revisit it on a regular basis.

This may be your homework. You may have to approach your financial advisor or insurance professional and say, "I want to talk about this. I need to talk about this." If they are fully on board and discuss information with you that has several different financial scenarios that might work for you, then it is likely that you are working with a professional that has your best interests at heart. If your financial advisor is a fiduciary, they owe you a duty. This is what fiduciary means. Ask them if they are a fiduciary and what does that mean to them? And tell them what it means to you.

Here are the questions you need to ask yourself and your financial advisor or insurance professional.

1. Can we talk about how an illness may affect our savings plan?
2. Am I prepared for that?
3. Do I need/have the right legal documents?
4. What would your company/investment company require if I am disabled for my loved ones to get to my money?
5. What is the cost of care in our area if I become sick or disabled chronically or permanently?
6. How am I going to pay for that? If we are a married couple, how are we going to pay for care AND keep money for the healthy spouse?
7. Can you tell me what we are going to do if my spouse, who has the bulk of our assets in his/her IRA, gets sick or disabled?
8. Since my spouse is the sole owner of that IRA, how am I as the spouse with no significant IRA going to be protected from a crisis of illness, how am I going to get money if that money is considered my spouse's money for paying for nursing home expenses.
9. How many different ways are there to create a long-term care plan? Long-term care insurance, hybrid policies, policies at my

work or my husband's work, self-insurance? What is a worst-case scenario?

10. Do you work with an Elder Lawyer, Insurance professional, Accountant that works in these areas? How does your company train you to educate about long-term care issues and crises from a financial point of view?

My sincerest hope is that if your financial advisor can't answer these questions to your satisfaction, they will tell you so. Perhaps you can work together to get all the necessary advice and expertise, or perhaps you need to get a different financial advisor. Look, there isn't one professional in any of these areas who can know everything. That's why you need to have your team of experts work together. If you have someone on your team who doesn't want to do that, they don't belong on your team.

These same questions can be used with your spouse and/or partner as well as your insurance professional. None of this means you can't do your own homework. You should. Ask around. Look up the cost of care in your area for home care, assisted living, or nursing homes. Get the Genworth Cost of Care App. It's an app that tells you, yep, the cost of care in your area by zip code. A great starting point. If your financial advisor does not know the cost of care in your area, you must.

If you don't have a financial professional or an insurance professional, ask yourself these questions:

1. Am I prepared for a medical crisis, either for myself or a family member that will have an impact on me and my life?
2. Do I have my legal documents so that I can have someone take care of me and have access to my finances if need be?
3. Does that family member I may have to care for have those documents so I can take care of them in a financially responsible way for them and me?

4. Am I prepared for the cost of long-term medical care? Either as the one being cared for or as a caregiver? Is there a cost of quitting work, losing income, or social security and retirement funds that go along with caregiving that I am prepared for?

5. What kind of long-term care do I want, home care, or a facility or a combination?

6. Have I researched the cost?

7. Is there anything I can do about the cost?

    a. Can I buy any kind of insurance product? Have I spoken to an insurance professional?

    b. Does my employer have any benefit I can purchase or look into?

    c. Does my family member have any long-term care insurance, policy, hybrid policy that might pay me as a caregiver as well as for additional care for them?

8. If I have prepared a financial plan, is it enough to pay for the kind of care I want?

9. If I have a loved one who is depending on me if they need care, what kind of care do they want?

10. Has a loved one who thinks they will depend on me prepared a financial plan for the cost of care that they want?

The reason I have included these questions for you and your long-term care issues is obvious. But the reason I have included a "loved one" here is that it is very often the piece that is sorely overlooked. Women (mostly women) who end up being caregivers, often end up having a financial crash. Women will give up jobs, social security, retirement benefits, job advancement and their own cash to take care of a loved one. Financial issues are rampant around caregiving and are the least talked about. Nobody asks the caregiver: Can you afford this? Can you afford to be a caregiver for a loved one?

A "loved one" covers a lot of bases. I was a caregiver for my brother-in-law and one of my best friends. The answers to these questions should be as important to you, if you are the caregiver, as they are to you or your mom, dad, grandmom or sister wondering how to pay for your own cost of care. If you or your loved one is acting as their own financial advisor, you need to look at these questions and answers seriously. If need be, then get help.

CHAPTER ELEVEN

A CONVERSATION WITH THE CAREGIVER

It's important to dispel the rumor that you are or are not a caregiver. As we said, if you take mom to the doctor and get her prescriptions and groceries, you're a caregiver. If you are a spouse and your husband or wife are ill, you're still a spouse, but you are also a caregiver. This chapter is a bit about you. If you see yourself in this chapter, and you need a two-by-four upside the head to accept some things, and give you power to do other things then here's your permission and your gift.

There are also paid caregivers. Caregivers who you hire to come to your home, or your parents' home to help you the *primary caregiver* (yup, you're still a caregiver even if you live 2,000 miles away, but you're in charge!) get your job accomplished.

The estimated nearly half a million home care agencies in the United States...yes...*half a million*, would indicate that many of you are working with hired caregivers. And although this book is largely dedicated to those dedicated unpaid caregivers, guess who is employing, hiring, firing, communicating with and begging those paid caregivers to do their job? Yes, the unpaid caregivers.

Let's begin this chapter (yes, we're just starting now, the other stuff was preamble!) with how to deal with the challenges of the paid caregiver. If you are fortunate enough to have created a financial situation where you can have paid caregivers come in, then you will have a different set of issues. Now you are an employer. If you are very lucky and I believe very prepared, you can have paid caregivers who will make your life easier and make your caregivee's life better.

There could be an entire book of sample conversations of all the challenges a paid caregiver will bring into your loved one's life. You are very different people with very different ideas about how to do things as simple as wash the dishes, or the laundry and as complex as how to talk to Dad when he is being uncooperative, difficult and downright rude. But you and the caregiver must set boundaries and have ideas about how to handle the hard parts and the easy parts.

Here are some ground rules, necessary conversations, and ideas for helping the paid caregiver relationship run smoothly with you, the unpaid, yet harried caregiver extraordinaire!

1. Why are you hiring a caregiver?

    Are you hiring someone to do cleaning, cooking, and laundry all the while being a companion to Mom? Or as it was in my case, someone to just come in, get my brother-in-law ready for the morning, check on him at noon time and put him to bed at night because he needed a Hoyer lift to get in and out of bed and help with his medications?

    There are thousands of reasons to hire caregivers. Before you do so write down exactly what you expect this person to do. Your needs can change over time, that's fine. This is not a tablet from Moses. But if you start out with clear expectations, then you and the caregiver can design their day and you won't be frustrated that the laundry wasn't done, the dishes weren't washed and Dad didn't get a shower that day.

No one is a mind reader here. And you are so attuned to what you want to do and when you want to do it, that you think everyone thinks like you. That's not how it works, so prepare yourself to be specific even before you hire your new right-hand person.

Because you could be hiring for so many reasons, in the beginning, be prepared for how you will deal with change. From the start it makes sense to clearly state this is a trial period, not for the caregiver, but for their duties. That way they are not immediately offended or worried that they will lose their job, the onus is on you to decide if you want them to do more or less duties. My personal experience is that the more you like your hired caregiver, the more you will be willing to give them expanded responsibility. Of course, your caregivee needs to like them, too. Once you are fortunate enough to have a symbiotic relationship going between your hired caregiver and your loved one....well, the sky's the limit!!!

Now you've made a list for the things you need a caregiver to do.

2. Get some advice.
   If you know of anyone who has hired caregivers ask them who they used to hire an in-home caregiver. The more personal references you obtain, the more you will get a feel for the kind of caregivers a home health agency hires.

   If you are a thousand miles away then it is just a matter of homework and research. There are Certified

Caregiving Consultants like those trained by my friend, the highly regarded, Denise Brown at https://www.careyearsacademy.com/ and Geriatric Counselors all over the country now. They can assist you in the research and retention of what you need for your loved one who lives far away. Do not hesitate to ask the agency for references of other customers, especially if you are not physically close. If you are physically close, you will want to interview the caregiver. But you can still use a Caregiving Consultant to assist you, why not? No need to re-invent the wheel.

Depending on your caregivee's situation, it may or may not be a good idea to include them in the interview process. I'm going to leave that up to you. You know your caregivee better than anyone:

- will they be open-minded
- amenable to outside help
- do they have prejudices that will be a problem for the caregiver

This is rarely discussed because it is sensitive. I can only tell you my personal experience, which is I didn't pay one bit of attention to my loved one's prejudices. My loved ones were mostly old people with issues and some long-standing prejudices, but not always. Sometimes, my younger, but ill, caregivees had issues that reared their ugly heads. I made sure my loved one treated each and every one of their caregivers with respect. The one or two times my caregivee was inappropriate or disrespectful to a hired caregiver, even if it was in a facility where I had no control over the employees, I took my loved one out to the woodshed. You know what

I mean. Caregiving is hard. I expected my loved ones to be treated with respect and I expected my loved ones to treat others the same way. If you haven't figured it out by now, I am mostly a "tough love" caregiver. That's me and that's my situation. The very critical point here is you are putting someone in a room with your loved one. Nobody needs to come out with bruises, physical or emotional…nobody. You're in charge. Pay attention to the things people call "emotional intelligence" and the rest of us call basic decency.

3.   Keep the lines of communication open.

Make sure your hired caregiver knows they can and should talk to you. Of course, your hired caregiver has a boss from the agency. Making all the issues go directly through the agency is probably not productive. There are going to be times when it is necessary to call in the big guns. And there are going to be times that the big guns are going to call you and/or your loved one on the carpet for the way a hired caregiver is treated. The more you communicate with the hired caregiver, the better it will be. If you are physically there to turn over the reins or check in with your hired caregiver, it's a good time to have a chat each day. Again, show respect. If you can spare the time for a cup of tea with the caregiver, that may be the best thing you can do.

If you are a long-distance caregiver then a daily or every other day call is likely a good idea. Once a week is not enough, that's how bad things happen. If the caregiver knows you are really involved, that you are interested in what they are seeing, that you are communicating with your loved one as well on a very regular basis, the more you will glean from what is going on. Nanny cams have evolved to Portal. There are dozens of ways to stay in touch with your loved one and their caregiver with technology today. But you are ultimately the human at the other end who will need to communicate with everyone.

4. Don't be afraid to fire people who aren't the right fit.
   It's hard, I know. You have someone in place. You don't want to do this hiring all over again. The wrong fit is the wrong fit. Cut your losses, because one way or another it's not going to work out. If you like the agency but not the worker, call the agency. If you don't like the agency, get another one. This is a pain in the tushy. I know. It's like finding the right therapist or hairdresser. It can take a few tries. I can only make it a bit easier by giving you some questions to ask.

5. Here's a thought…tell people when they are doing a good job!
   If you, yourself have been doing all the heavy lifting for a week, a month, a decade, you know how nice it is to hear you are doing a good job. Sure, your hired caregiver gets paid, but it's always nice to hear that you are appreciated and doing a good job. Once you are lucky enough to find that gem of a caregiver who you trust, who your mother loves, who never lets you down, don't be stingy with the praise. It matters and you know it.

Questions to ask a Hired Caregiver:

There are dozens of questions you can ask and I will keep it simple here, but I would like you to go online and Google this as well for two reasons. One, there are several really good resources out there with lists of questions. Two, since every situation is different, you will find in all those countless resources some questions that apply to your situation that you may not have considered. The questions I have here are outside of the name, address, etc. demographic information that you may need, especially if you are hiring without an agency. You need that basic information, but for brevity, I wanted to concentrate on the meatier questions that truly need answering and that many caregiver websites have come to the conclusion are critical for you to know before making a decision.

1. How long have you been doing caregiving work?
2. Are you able to do lifting to help my loved one in and out of bed, chairs, etc.?
3. Do you smoke?
4. Do you drive? Do you have transportation?
5. Do you have other clients?
6. Are you willing to sign an addition to our contract that you will not accept money or gifts from my loved one?
7. Do you have flexibility to extend your time with my loved one?
8. Do you know how to cook?
9. Have you cared for someone with my loved one's issues in the past?
10. Can I get references from three of your previous or current clients?

The big take away here is that you must have a lengthy conversation about your needs. You must have a contract. And you can find various contracts on line that meet your needs, if you are not using an agency. You must make certain that conversations with your caregiver are continuous.

It would be helpful to take a page out of corporate America and have a weekly Wednesday meeting with your caregiver to discuss concerns, ideas and note what is going well. Stress, crisis, illness are all the enemies of open communication. We are all so wrapped up in medications, doctor's appointments, durable medical equipment, urinary tract infections, and a million other minute, yet important details of caregiving that we ignore communication. And especially in this chapter, where we may very well be engaging with someone whose communications styles are vastly different from our own, we need to be cognizant of keeping those conversations going.

Conversations. The Title of this Book. Not talking AT your caregiver. Not telling them what to do and how to do it. Not complaining about what isn't done. Yes, you will do those things but the conversing part is just as critical. Conversing with them about how to make this work for your loved one, for you and for your caregiver. The last thing you want is to be hiring caregivers every two weeks. It's going to happen, but if you're lucky, like I was, you may find a core group of caregivers who stick with you for years.

This is not to say that you will not need to air your complaints. You have to make it clear, concise and not accusatory if it's a caregiver you want to keep. If you want to fire them, then fine. If this is just you being you, where you need to get things done, then look at this relationship as a real employer, if necessary. Would you want to be your own employee? Then treat the caregiver that way. If you're fortunate enough to have a caregiver situation that your loved one is enjoying and you are too, foster that in a way where you can continue it but still get what you need as the primary caregiver. It's easier to say to a hired caregiver: "We meet every Wednesday at 10 AM to discuss how the week went so that we can continue to stay on the same page about my father's care." It's almost impossible to say that to your sister or brother. Family would be : "Oh, for crying out loud, *every* week? Can't you just call me? Wednesday is my poker night?" Let's be thankful for this hired relationship. It may be easier than family!

CHAPTER TWELVE

A CONVERSATION WITH WORK

This one is going to be a surprise to a lot of people. If you are an employee and a caregiver, you may be surprised what your employer has for you to help you with this caregiving life. If you are an employer, you may be surprised that you have caregiving employees. You may be a caregiver yourself.

You, as an employer, may be surprised and gratified to find that you already have some benefits in place that you and your employees were unaware of. As an employer you may want to create some caregiving benefits for your trusted employees. You may be thinking you can't afford to do that. You may find that you can't afford NOT to include caregivers in creating a better workplace. Let's take a look at both of you!

EMPLOYEES

How to talk to my employer about being a caregiver:

Why do you need to talk to your employer about caregiving? Well, my friends, I hate to tell you this but it's not a secret. If you are deep in caregiving, everyone knows it. Even if you are working from home, many people became instantaneous caregivers for kids, elderly parents, and other relatives who now needed someone to be in charge in the year 2020.

If you are just dabbling in caregiving, meaning you either don't think you're a caregiver because you are "only taking your mom to the doctor's office, doing Aunt Minnie's grocery shopping, or picking up Dad's prescriptions," you are indeed a caregiver. Just because you are a daughter, son, spouse, or sibling doesn't mean you are not a caregiver. And you still need some support in the workplace.

Oddly, in some ways a pandemic has given many employees the ability to work flexibly around their caregiving issues. If you were caregiving for your parents before the pandemic, becoming a work-from-home (now known as WFH) employee may have become a bonus. You now had flexibility without worrying that you had to leave your office space.

But if you suddenly had kids at home, couldn't see your parents, were trying to Instacart for your family and your parents, were sleeping less because everyone is around all the time, well, yeah, caregiving and work became next to impossible. And yet, many of us discovered that being a WFH employee gave us some caregiving benefits that we cannot easily give up.

You may think this is not your employers' problem, that it's your problem. But what if your employer is having the same problem with everyone? Like, everyone?!? How many employees are struggling with this? So many. What does that mean for your employer? They are dealing with a work force that is not at 100 percent. If we give this a cold, hard look, perhaps we can help both the employer and the employee to make this caregiving thing a challenge to be dealt with but not a cherry bomb waiting to go off at every corner that leaves the employer high and dry when all the caregivers up and quit. This is what happened in 2020. It's estimated that two million women, yes, 2,000,000…left the workforce during the Covid crisis. It might now be as high as three million. If you don't think that negatively impacted employers, you would be kidding yourself.

The impact of loss of employees on a large scale due to caregiving responsibilities has brought to light the need to bring this issue to the forefront and deal with it. Employers and employees must find solutions to the problem of caregiving that has been swept under the carpet for years. We know this because before the Covid pandemic there were an estimated 44 million to 66 million unpaid caregivers. These are unpaid caregivers. This does not mean they are unpaid people. It means they are unpaid for caregiving. In the meantime, many of them are working somewhere else. Employers are paying those unpaid caregivers, to do their paid job while they are trying to juggle caregiving.

This is why the conversation with your employer seems so difficult. You know that you have to tattle on yourself about how hard your life is. You believe that you shouldn't get or don't deserve special treatment. More importantly, you really believe that if you broach the subject of caregiving with your employer as a problem that needs some solutions, the easiest solution will be that you are no longer employed. I can't promise that won't happen. But I can tell you that for lots of reasons practical, legal and moral, employers are stepping up to the plate in new and interesting ways. I can also tell you that caregiving for elderly parents, disabled spouses, siblings or even friends is now the "dirty little secret," that childcare used to be.

There was a time when women wouldn't even think about asking for any kind of accommodations for childcare issues. But that ship has sailed. Not everywhere, mind you. We still have a way to go, which is why those million moms and caregivers had to leave the workforce during a pandemic. We still aren't up to snuff here in the United States for making caregiving a priority. But we are getting closer every day. Real inroads are being made both corporately and legislatively to make this a challenge we can all turn into an opportunity for good work for everyone,

Okay, all that being said. How do you talk to your employer?

131

First, you have some homework to do. Generally, if you work for an employer with over fifty employees, you have benefits under the Family and Medical Leave Act, better known as the FMLA. As of this writing, those benefits are 12 unpaid weeks and are restricted to care for self, spouses, children or parents. However, also at this writing, the current administration is trying to extend that leave to additional persons AND create a paid leave policy. That would be amazing, and I have high hopes for those changes.

But the real question is "What does YOUR EMPLOYER DO?" Many companies of all sizes have leave for family issues. Some have leave under the American with Disabilities Act if you are the one who is suffering from the disability. Some have paid leave, some have shared leave where your fellow employees can donate their leave to your "bucket of benefits," so to speak. Some employers have unpaid leave. Some companies allow you to purchase short-term and long-term disability policies. Some of those long-term policies can be purchased for other family members like parents. The list of possibilities is endless, and you need to find out if your employer has any options for you.

There will be a list of questions to ask in this chapter. But I need to give you a caveat: many an employer and/or HR professional has no idea if there are caregiving benefits at work. They may be familiar with FMLA, or they may not. Your company might be too small for FMLA. So, the answer may be: "we're too small for FMLA." That does not mean there are not any benefits. Often, a company's health insurance provider may have some hidden gems that no one has ever bothered to investigate. There are health insurance programs that have adult day care stipends, health club stipends (for a caregiver who needs a break, like a yoga class!), the aforementioned long-term care benefits for one's self, spouse or parents that an employee can purchase. Some companies have legal services as a part of the benefits package. Those legal services at a discounted rate can be invaluable to a caregiver who needs to have Powers of Attorney, Living Wills or even Wills drawn up in crisis situations.

Rhode Island, California and New Jersey have paid family leave programs that provide four to six weeks of paid leave through a Temporary Caregiver Insurance program funded by payroll deductions. So, you may very well be paying for a caregiver benefit that you didn't know you had! Washington State is implementing a long-term care insurance plan as we speak. And New York State is considering one of the most comprehensive caregiver initiatives to pay for caregiving leave that would exist. Conversely, six states, California, Connecticut, Illinois, Oregon, Vermont, Massachusetts and 19 cities have mandated paid sick leave, which for caregivers is "not nuthin" as my Pop Pop would say. That's because caregivers' health is often compromised to the point where their own sick leave is critical. This is where the ADA can also come into play, for one's own care. Or honestly, you may not know that your sick spouse is entitled to ADA accommodations from *their* work, if you are the caregiver of a spouse. It's a crazy quilt of possible benefits that employers may be required to provide, already exist and/or things they do not even know about that employees may be grateful to have.

I have been fortunate to work with digital platforms that provide employee benefits solely for caregiving. Some employers have purchased these digital platforms, some health insurance companies have a very similar platform as part of health insurance benefits. One of my favorite innovative platforms is TCARE®. It is a tailored caregiver assessment and referral platform. TCARE® provides triage and management care programs for caregiver references and services and has been implemented in over 13 states. Based on data research, TCARE® has proven that taking care of *caregivers* actually is more cost effective to Medicare and Medicaid, saving thousands if not millions of dollars in governmental services. TCARE® is expanding every day and their data continues to support the notion that finding resources for caregivers that make the caregiving job easier will be a profitable benefit to employers everywhere.

Ali Ahmed, the CEO of TCARE® and I had a chat that I think you might find interesting. I asked Ali to complete the answers to seven statements I created. Here are my questions and his answers. I believe every employer can benefit from the philosophy of this company as well as the action it is taking to improve the workplace by improving the lives of caregivers:

1. We created TCARE® because:

    My personal experience as a caregiver for my mother-in-law inspired the creation of TCARE®. I saw that there were no targeted resources for us as a family. There was only a "shot-gun" approach to providing a menu of possible resources that might assist us in our caregiving journey. It was confusing and time-consuming creating further stress to the caregivers. I recognized that (as a former military guy) we needed a 'sniper approach' to help the caregiver pin-point the resources they specifically needed. And that would require data.

2. We found and continue to find:

    It is not the physical needs of the elder or the extensive hours of care that lead to caregiver burnout. We continue to find that the emotional and psycho-social stress rather than the physical stress is what leads to caregiver burnout and ultimately to higher caregiver costs both for the elder and the caregiver.

3. We are using TCARE® in the governmental sector now because:

We knew there was a lack of *caregiver* support in all governmental programs for long-term care issues, especially for what is labeled HCBS, which is Home and Community Based Services. By creating a longitudinal study of the caregiver rather than the person they were caring for, we have identified the root causes of caregiver burnout. By using that same data to precision target the specific needs of a caregiver to prevent that burnout, we have been able to create, sustain and fund targeted services for caregivers and their families, that based on data, saves money for governmental resources. Additionally, the same targeted needs program uncovers new governmental resources available for families that were previously unheard of our unused. So, for example, if you look at it from both sides, we save money for Medicaid by not having to put someone in a nursing home, and we use resources in a waiver program that are going unused because families weren't aware that they qualified for such resources. And if you want to extend it even further, by keeping a caregiver healthy and providing resources that address their emotional and psycho-social needs they are using less health care visits as their physical and mental health are not being as adversely affected by caregiving.

4. We can see a future in the corporate sector because of:
   Our ROI, return on investment outcomes for an employer are proven. This is all across the board, Medicare, Medicaid, private health plans, commercial health plans and self-insured employer health plans all save money by investing in a TCARE® plan. (This is me: If it's money we're talking about saving, Ali has the

data to prove that it is happening when you address the caregiving problem and take care of caregivers!)

5. Generally, we believe that taking care of caregivers is profitable for employers because:

   It reduces absenteeism, it increases presenteeism, it significantly reduces employee turnover which saves the cost of retraining.

6. Caregivers are not going away based on our data which finds:

   The number of caregivers is growing exponentially every day. We see the numbers growing in double digits up to the year 2050. No, caregivers are not going away. Awareness of this challenge in the workplace is critical.

7. Personally, in our company we give caregivers:

   Our staff has unlimited paid time off (PTO), that was our first response to this. Our employees work with caregivers every day and so they and we are very aware of the impact of this challenge on work life. In addition, we have flexibility not just for work from home (WFH) but for the hours in a day where you may need flexibility to address caregiving issues.

Okay, I did ask Ali one more question because I find that my clients, my friends, my acquaintances continue to voice the "I'm afraid to bring this up at work..." conversation. So, I asked Ali:

"Are you certain that your employees are asking for all the support they need as caregivers, and are they afraid to broach the subject?"

Here's what he said:

It is only an employer's stupidity that refuses to be sympathetic to the plight of the caregiver. If there are ways to effectuate productivity and keep good employees, why would you foster an environment where they are afraid to talk to you? This is how it used to be for childcare and now there are many companies, large and small that have childcare right in the workplace. No, our employees are not afraid to discuss this and we encourage them to let us know how we can help. We believe caregiving is a badge of honor and our employees know that we are supportive of them in every possible way.

I'm not kidding when I tell you I had tears in my eyes and a catch in my throat. It's so important to unpaid working caregivers to know that they can get through this and not lose everything they have worked for.

So………

There are other platforms as well that may be a part of your health insurance, your Employee Assistance Program (EAP), some of these things are provided by companies like Anthem, Blue Cross/Blue Shield, Torchlight, and Wellthy for example.

What do these platforms do? They may help you contact governmental agencies that provide benefits for your loved one. They may connect you with lawyers, social workers, nursing homes, assisted living facilities or home care agencies. TCARE® provides specific resources locally, if necessary for the caregiver, herself.

All of this would take the place of you, an employee spending her time either during the confines of work hours, or after work if that's even possible, when you're already exhausted, trying to get this information and these services for your sick loved one or even yourself. Good luck trying to call a home care provider or agency for information at ten o'clock at night.

These are just a sampling of all the kinds of things an employer can do to improve the employee/caregiver situation. It is also a sampling of the kinds of benefits that are often in place for employees that no one knows about, or knows how to access. Crazy, right?

So how do we approach this? By checking your benefits book. Yes, that thing that nobody ever reads. Whether it is online or an actual book, you've got to read it cover to cover. Then ask questions of your boss, your HR, your benefits provider/healthcare insurance provider. Once you've had these conversations with any and all of these people about how to implement anything that you found in the handbook to help you, you begin to help yourself and the dozens of other employees at your job who are having similar issues.

My wildest dream is that these 'difficult' conversations at work or with HR are going to become a thing of the past...not the conversation, the difficulty. One way or another, if caregiving is going to become a big or even small part of your life, why wouldn't you want to know what your employer has in place to retain you and help you through this all the while being a good employee.

Here are some ways to start the conversation and some of the questions you can ask as an employee:

Terri: Boss, I need to have a conversation.

Boss: Uh oh. What happened now? Did Ron make inappropriate remarks, again? I have had words with him, Terri, I promise.

Terri: No Boss, Ron is actually behaving. We are all surprised. No this is completely different and completely personal.

Boss: Oh, gee. What is it, Terri?

Terri: Well, you know my mother has been quite ill.

Boss: Yes, I was hoping she was doing better.

Terri: Unfortunately, that hasn't happened. In fact, we had to move her in with us.

Boss: Oh, Terri. That is unfortunate.

Terri: Yeah, so it's been pretty difficult. I'm going to need some help.

Boss: Oh, okay. So, what are you thinking?

This is where it would behoove you to have a plan. Before you meet with your boss or HR you should think about what you truly need.

Here are three questions that can help you prepare:

1. What do I need to help me do my job and caregiving without losing my mind or my job?
   a. More flexibility? For example, I can do some of my work outside of office hours so that I can be with my kids to help with virtual school, help my disabled mother to give her a bath, meds, take her to the doctor, etc. Are you okay with that? That means I am unavailable from 1:00 to 3:00 every day.
      Start with what you need ideally.
   b. Help with resources. Do we have health insurance benefits, an EAP or anything in place I can use to help with caregiving responsibility?
   c. Do we have FMLA for my situation? Is it paid?
   d. Nobody knows better than you what you need. If you are living with a partner ask them too, what *they* think *you* need. And if they are also working, ask them what you both need as caregiving partners.

139

Maybe they see things you don't see when it comes to required help. Maybe they have something at their job that will help you!

2. I've done some research on what the company has. I think this would help me. Do you know if there is anything I am missing?

   a. I would tell whomever you're speaking to what you found. Or that you found nothing, which wouldn't be weird.

3. I do not want to lose my job just because I am a caregiver. Have you worked with caregivers before, how did the company work with them in the past?

   a. Now that Covid has changed the landscape of caregiving, especially with childcare, have we as a company put anything in place for individuals that I should know about now that I am asking? Oh, and I may or may not be talking about caregiving for children, but the problem is the same.

   Let's not be so naïve as to think that an employer may be working with individual employees who have brought up this problem. The employer may have been willing to help solve the problem, especially for an employee they wish to retain, and not shared with others the accommodations that have been made. It doesn't mean you are being ignored, but it probably does mean you and many others haven't asked for help.

So now you have approached this problem with work. You have had a conversation about the fact that you are in a caregiving situation. Here are some of the questions you can pursue and also, depending on your place in the company, here are some ideas you can provide to your employer and fellow employees. And don't think, well I'm just an admin in the HR office, or I am in engineering which has nothing to do with this. Are you connected to the Women's Group or the Diversity and Inclusion Group? Are you in the Events Group and can bring people like me in to talk to your employer (that seems like shameless self-promotion and maybe it is a little bit, but truthfully, it is something you can do!)

Also, might I add that if you are in HR or on any of those committees, or involved with your Employee Assistance Program (EAP) or anything like that and you are NOT a caregiver, you still can bring this to your employer. It's important. It's a hot topic in employment. It may just make you be seen as the forward-thinking, thought leader you truly are at work!

Ten Questions to ask your employer/HR about the caregiving dilemma:

1. Can I have a conversation about caregiving issues without being afraid of losing my job?
2. Has anyone ever come to you before with this problem? Not because I want to know their name. I want to know if this is a unique problem.
3. Do you know if we have any resources to help with my caregiving issues?

   Of course, you will need to tell them what your issues are and what resources you may need, but you may be surprised that HR might have knowledge of resources you didn't even know you needed.
4. Do we have the capability for more flexibility?
5. Can we discuss some temporary solutions while we work this out?
6. Is there an actual corporate plan in place for caregiving issues?

7. Do we have federally mandated benefits such as Family and Medical Leave Act (FMLA)?

8. Does our Health Insurance plan have extraordinary or supplemental benefits that would help a caregiver? e.g. A digital platform about caregiving services, legal services, long-term care insurance, adult day care subsidies, consultation services for elder care with geriatric counselors, home care agencies, assisted living agencies, telemedicine.

9. If we don't have anything that you are aware of, should I meet with HR?

10. Can we look at what I need and then maybe see how it can be used to help other caregivers?

EMPLOYER

Now it's time to take a look at yourself, Employer. Why should you look at the caregiving monolith as something that you should care about? I mean, why isn't this just the caregiver's problem? It's their family and I'm not in the business of dealing with my employee's family problems. I'm in the business of widgets. My employees come here to make widgets. I pay them well. We have health insurance and IRA's. They get vacation and holidays. I'm a good employer.

Yes, you are a good employer. You are going above and beyond. Your employees are happy to work for you. This is the best-case scenario. Yet, with 44 million to 66 million unpaid caregivers out there, these caregivers are working for you. You may or may not know that. That may not be your fault. It is well-known in the caregiving community that caregivers fail to self-identify. It is also well-known that it's rare to have anyone asking the question at work, "are you a caregiver?" There will be no assigning of blame here. That serves no one. What we will try and do is show you how it is to your benefit to identify and help those caregivers be better employees by helping them with that caregiving stuff. It seems counter-intuitive to provide more, but if you have caregivers, and you do, you will get more if you give them an assist with this caregiving thing.

This book is being written during and after months of a worldwide pandemic. That gives us a certain point of view. If we are being honest, unpaid caregiving has been a deep problem for many years prior to this pandemic. With ten thousand Baby Boomers turning 65 years-old every day in this country, we have been under a caregiving burden for generations. And then, on top of that a quarter of the millions of unpaid caregivers are millennials. Those adults, started out as kids, maybe even kids of caregivers. Just know that this has been going on for generations and it's time to take a serious look at how work and caregiving need to get along for the benefit of everyone. I am the eternal optimist. I know it can be done.

THE STEPS FOR AN EMPLOYER TO IMPROVE THE WORKPLACE BY HELPING CAREGIVERS

You have to want to.

Or do you? I believe this is coming to your door in one way or another. If you reject that this is an employment issue, I need to share some information with you.

THE STATISTICS:

I have chosen three sets of statistical information that I think may convince you that this is an area of the workplace that not only needs improvement, but can improve your bottom line if done with what we in Catholic school called the Seven Gifts of the Holy Spirit: Wisdom, Understanding, Counsel, Fortitude, Knowledge, Piety and Fear of the Lord!

I promise not to glaze your eyes over with a bunch of numbers and charts, you can go to the referenced sources for that delight. What I am going to do here is show you how this is having an impact on your business and what you can do about it.

1. THE WASHINGTON STUDY:

Several years ago, the State of Washington undertook a study to look at the impact of caregiving on caregivers and how improving their situation could improve the actual cost of caregiving to the state. The results were remarkable. The study indicated that by improving a caregiver's life, the cost of services to the state for a person requiring care would actually cost less.

Here is the summary:

Data used for this report were obtained from the Washington State Department of Social and Health
Services (DSHS) Aging and Long-Term Support Administration (ALTSA) were taken from records for
caregivers participating in the Family Caregiver Support Program (FCSP). The data were collected via the
use of the Tailored Caregiver Assessment and Referral® (TCARE®) system assessment tool between
March 2010 and December 2013.

Key Findings:
• 84% of caregivers who remained in the program for six months reported improved levels of stress and depression.
• The 16% of caregivers who did not show improvement were providing more assistance of all types and were caring for family members who engaged in more problem behaviors. There was also a decline in the functional level of the persons for whom they provide care.
• After 12 months of participation in the program, caregivers continued to have statistically significant lower levels of stress and depression than they did at the time of initial enrollment.
• As a group, caregivers who placed the care recipient in a long-term care facility prior to the six-month follow-up had the highest levels of stress and depression at the time of the of the initial assessment. Their scores on all measures of stress and depression were higher than those of caregivers who

continued in the program and those of caregivers whose care recipient died prior to the six-month follow up.

• The group of caregivers whose care recipient died prior to the six-month follow-up was providing the most assistance for care recipients with the greatest functional impairment, but did not have higher levels of stress. They had the lowest scores of relationship burden and the highest levels of uplifts or positive feelings about caregiving.

A. Background

This report provides a summary of findings from analyses of records for 11,101 informal caregivers who participated in the Family Caregiver Support Program (FCSP) administered by the Aging and Long-Term Support Administration (ALTSA) in the Washington State Department of Social and Health Services. The Tailored Caregiver Assessment and Referral® (https://www.careyearsacademy.com/system was adopted by ALTSA in 2009 in response to a directive from the Washington State Legislature to identify and use an evidence based assessment and referral tool for use within the Family Caregiver Support Program (FCSP).**

**Report to the Washington Aging and Long-Term Support Administration: May 2014, Rhonda J.V. Montgomery, PH.D, Helen Bader School of Social Welfare, University of Wisconsin-Milwaukee

The study found that by providing a path for the caregiver to recognize the stress of her situation and take concrete action steps to remain healthy, the caregivee was less likely to end up in a facility. This is how the State of Washington saved money. It makes sense to extrapolate that acknowledging and assisting with caregiving challenges that affect the workplace steps to assist the caregiver will improve productivity and reduce health care costs of caregiver employees.

It is interesting to note that this year, the State of Washington has passed legislation that provides a long-term care benefit to all employed individuals which is funded by a payroll tax. It is not a significant benefit, only $36,500.00 which with the cost of care we discussed earlier wouldn't go too far. Yet, those funds can be used to pay caregivers who would likely be unpaid caregivers under most circumstances. This recognizes a shift in policy about the fact that long-term care costs and issues are becoming ubiquitous and must be acknowledged and dealt with as a cost for everyone.

2. TCARE®:

I am not yet finished with my friend Ali Ahmadi at TCARE®! Ali is the master of BIG DATA. He has taken a unique approach to caregiving as a place to look at data He wanted to see if helping the caregiver actually makes or saves money for someone. Here's what he specifically found:

> The study findings provide strong support for our main hypothesis that the use of the TCARE® protocol, which is designed to identify the unique needs of an individual caregiver and strategically recommend a set of services, will promote the well-being and mental health of caregivers.
>
> The types of services that the TCARE® protocol identifies as resources best aimed to reduce objective burden are adult day care and in-home homemaker or personal care services. These are also the types of services that are frequently made available to caregivers through usual care management practice...the present results provide initial support for the TCARE® protocol as an effective means to reduce multiple dimensions of caregiver burden and depression, which may also reduce the desire for institutionalization of care receivers.*

* Montgomery, R.J.V., Kwak, J., Kosloski, K., & O'Connell Valuch, K. (2011). Effects of the TCARE®) ® intervention on caregiver burden and depressive symptoms: preliminary findings from a randomized controlled study. *The Journals of Gerontology, Series B: Psychological Sciences and Social Sciences, 66(5)*, 640–647, doi:10.1093/geronb/gbr088

These numbers aren't even post-pandemic. This is before 2020 when caregiving was coming to the forefront. Some of the reasons are obvious, some are not. From an employer's point of view, I believe the most compelling information is that retaining and recruiting has become exponentially difficult and what employees are now looking for is anything you can offer for work life balance. Employees are quitting their jobs rather than going back to required office space. Employees will gladly give up raises for more paid vacation, more time off, more accommodations for child care, caregiving and personal time.

Employees are driving this desire to reevaluate the work model. I remember when my daughter was willing to give up a significant salary increase for three more weeks of paid vacation. This would actually have saved her potential employer 10 grand, easily. But, no, she was told. That was not possible. Why? Because that's not the way we've always done it. Others might be jealous. Blah, blah, blah. Time to take a new look, employers. You will be at the forefront. It's already here, but you can still be someone that employees are looking for. How does that sound? Your Human Resources department will thank you. You are going to be the one who can recruit and retain because you are looking at caregiving.

3. AARP and the NATIONAL ALLIANCE for CAREGIVING

AARP has taken the time to create a singular Caregiving arm to its already vast empire of information it provides to the aging population, their caregivers and families. Along with its newsletters, magazines, and websites with dedicated caregiver information, AARP has conducted research and published policy papers about work and the caregiver dilemma.

This is the Gold Standard for understanding how caregiving is affecting us all in every aspect of our lives. Even though AARP is "for retired people," this continuing comprehensive study which began over twenty years ago and has been conducted five times, includes caregivers of all ages and addresses the impact caregiving is having on the lives of unpaid caregivers, including in the work place.

Here are some of those findings from the last two studies in 2015 and 2020:

A. Understanding the Impact of Family Caregiving on Work: https://www.aarp.org/content/dam/aarp/research/public_p olicy_institute/ltc/2012/understanding-impact-family-caregiving-work-AARP-ppi-ltc.pdf

In this policy paper, authors Lynn Feinberg and Rita Choula delineate employees who are affected by caregiving by age group, by salaried or hourly employment and by age. The conclusions are irrefutable.

U.S. businesses lose up to an estimated $33.6 billion per year in lost productivity from full-time working caregivers. Costs associated with replacing employees, absenteeism, workday distractions, supervisory time, and reductions in hours from

full-time to part-time all take a toll. The average annual cost to employers per full-time working caregiver is $2,110. ***

***MetLife Mature Market Institute and National Alliance for Caregiving (NAC), *MetLife Caregiving Study: Productivity Losses to U.S. Business* (Westport, CT: MetLife Mature Market Institute, and Bethesda, MD: NAC, 2006). The lost productivity estimates are based on the 2004 survey of U.S. caregivers conducted by NAC and AARP, *Caregiving in the U.S. 2004*.

This is the obvious cost. If employers know that they have caregivers in their employ, they probably have experienced these challenges. Often, employers do not know that an employee is a caregiver, most often because employees fail to communicate that information to their employer. There are even hidden costs by way of health care issues that the caregiver, herself may be experiencing. From the same policy paper:

> *Research also shows a link between working caregivers with eldercare responsibilities and their health care costs.*
>
> ▪ *In one study, employers paid about 8 percent more for the health care of caregiver employees compared to noncaregivers, potentially costing U.S. businesses $13.4 billion per year.*
>
> ▪ *Both younger employees (age 18 to 39) and older employees (age 50+) with eldercare responsibilities were more likely to report fair or poor health in general.* ****

****MetLife Mature Market Institute, National Alliance for Caregiving, and University of Pittsburgh, *MetLife Study of Working Caregivers and Employer Health Care Costs* (Westport, CT: MetLife Mature Market Institute, February 2010).

So, what can an employer do? What should an employer do? The crux of the matter is that caregiving is here to stay. As 10,000 Baby Boomers a day turn 65, they continue to be caregivers for their elderly loved ones and it is likely that those coming after them will be caregiving for them. What does this mean to the work place? Caregiving is a tsunami to get in front of from an employers' point of view.

There are unquestionable benefits to an employer to who provides a caregiving friendly workplace. The money lost to re-hiring, re-training, and failure to provide flexibility, has been proven to be recouped with programs, education and resilience on the part of the employer. The truth of the matter is that sometimes it is the employer who needs to educate him/herself about productivity and how changing old habits can work for everyone.

Let's say you're convinced. You want to take an honest look at how to integrate your caregiver employees lives with their work lives so everybody wins.

A. Steps an Employer can take:

1. Ask yourself: Do you have any policies in place right now?
    - Maternity Leave
      If you do have a maternity leave policy, how can it be equally expanded to include caregivers for all ages?
    - Is it paid leave?
    - How many weeks is it?
    - Does it include fathers
    - Can it just be 'leave'?
    - Is your maternity leave longer than leave for other illnesses?

2. Look at your sick leave:
   - Do you have sick leave for illnesses other than maternity leave?
   - Why are they different?
   - Can sick leave be expanded to include the employee's family, not just the employee?
   - Is it paid leave?
   - Do you have a hybrid of paid and unpaid leave under any circumstances?
   - Do your higher paid employees have more leave benefits than your lower paid employees? Why?

3. Look at your flex time benefits:
   - Do you have scaled time for return to work? e.g. part-time leading to full-time return depending on leave status
   - Can employees have a more flexible schedule in general to accommodate caregiving needs?
   - If you have added flex-time to your schedule because of Covid-19 can you keep it? Have you asked employees how they feel about it?

4. Ask yourself: Do you know who your caregivers are?
   - Do you have any kind of way to determine if your employees are caregivers and need assistance?
   - When caregivers identify themselves, do you have a plan for how the company handles caregiving issues with employees?
   - Have you ever considered caregiving accommodations, benefits or initiatives within your company?

5. Ask yourself: Do you know what kind of caregiver accommodations other employers have put into place or are considering?

    - FMLA-some employers are required by law to offer 12 weeks of unpaid leave. Some have made it paid leave. Some have made it more than 12 weeks.

    - Exceeding FMLA guidelines:
      Some employers are not required to follow FMLA guidelines but provide leave anyway. Other employers extend FMLA outside of immediate family (get the FMLA allowable family members here)
      And then of course, whether it is paid or unpaid leave is also an employer's choice.

6. Look at Digital Platforms:
    - The rise of digital platforms to assist employees in the caregiving job while still being a good and effective employee is becoming ever more present and impressive.
    - Digital Platforms such as Torchlight and Wellthy and Genworth's Cost of Care App and Genworth's Caregiving platform are just a few examples of places where employers are freeing up an employees' time for research and help in caregiving by having an at-your-fingertips-assistant.

7. Check for an Employee Assistance Plans (EAPs):
    - You may have one or you may want to create one.
    - Your Health Insurer may have an EAP structure you would like to investigate.

8. Do you have a Women's Initiatives and Diversity and Inclusion Group?
   - Many companies have these groups
   - Have they discussed the Caregiving Issue?
   - Is this an initiative within their group that needs to be addressed on a higher level?

9. Can you bring in Health and Welfare Companies to the workplace?
   - Independent Health and Welfare companies are already in larger corporate spaces
     - Are your employees taking advantage of this benefit if you have it?
     - Is this an add-on benefit your company can/should consider?

10. Check Insurance Benefits: Adult Day Care, Legal Services, Long-term care insurance?
    - Would a benefits review show that you have some or all of these benefits already in place?
    - Is there merely an education factor lacking that can be resolved with some information, education or workshops?
    - Can you make these benefits available to your employees at little or no cost to you? (Hint: the answer is yes. If these benefits aren't already included in your insurance benefits, there are benefits providers who have things called Voluntary Benefits, where an employee can bear the cost.)

11. Check Job sharing and Benefits sharing
    - A flexible benefit created a very long time ago where employees actually help one another. If this

benefit existed in your company and has gone by the wayside perhaps you should consider re-establishing something that works and can work for you.

12. Does a dedicated HR employee for Caregiving Issues make sense?

- The reason caregiving has such a negative impact on work is that no one knows who to talk to, what the rules are, how it is dealt with, what is in place to help the employer and the employee. If you are becoming an employer who is seen as one who values work-life balance, a dedicated HR person to handle these issues will make you a cut above. It will dispel the fear of discussing this caregiving/work thing and it will help your employee consider staying not straying.

B. Questions that will help an Employer decide if taking a positive approach to caregiving is an important employee benefit?

1. Do we have a caregiving issue?
2. Are we aware of employees dealing with caregiving issues?
   a. Should we find that out?
   b. How do we do that?
   c. How are other companies doing that?
3. If we do have this issue, how are we dealing with it?
   a. Is it on a case-by-case basis? If so, is that the most effective way?
   b. Are we open to this caregiver conversation or do we wait for it to happen?

      c.   Are HR and management aligned with how we deal with this?

      d.   Have we ever had a management meeting about how to deal with this?

4.   Do we have corporate solutions in place?

      a.   Are there benefits at our workplace that are required by law?

          e.g. Family and Medical Leave Act (FMLA)

      b.   Do we have benefits that are in place from our health care insurance provider?

          e.g. Legal Services, Adult Day Care Benefits, Long-Term Care insurance for employees and their family members?

      c.   Does anybody know what they are?

      d.   Have we provided accommodations or solutions to some employees and not others? If so, is that legal? Should we look at that?

      e.   Does our Employee Assistance Program (EAP) have solutions that we are not using?

      f.   Have we proactively taken any steps? Digital platforms, Assistance Platforms with our health care insurance?

The hard data shows that by supporting the caregiver, work gets better and work gets done. But there is an even greater benefit to the employer. The cost to retrain goes down because the cost to retain caregivers with some supports is far less than hiring and training new people. In some ways, "the great experiment of 2020" due to COVID-19 requiring nearly the entire workforce to work from home opened our eyes to the fact that employees can be trusted to be even more productive from their home base. The lie that employees are less productive because you aren't literally looking at them all day long has been dispelled and it needs to stay that way. This opens the door for a work place that is productive and compassionate. That is a workplace where employees want to stay. HR will thank you for that, because ultimately, it makes their job easier.

I am not suggesting this is an overnight fix. Some work and thought needs to go into how to create the new normal where caregiving is recognized and treated as a challenge for employer and employee alike. But I am suggesting that it isn't really that difficult to see what you already have in place to help employees, to add some benefits that will ultimately help you, the employer, and to create a work force and a work place that has people there who want to stay, even in challenging times. As a caregiver for eight different family members and friends, I want you to know that the caregiving journey does end, and when it does, both employee and employer alike benefit from having navigated that journey together and successfully. It's not just me saying that, the stats say that too.

CHAPTER THIRTEEN

AIN'T NO SHAME IN LAUGHING!

If you're familiar with my work, you know that I am all about looking at the comedic side of caregiving. What?!?! You, say! If you are already a caregiver or have needed even short-term caregiving after you broke your leg when you fell while 'power-walking,' like my mom did when she was 86 and insisted, she had a 'sports injury' not an old lady injury of a broken hip, then you know caregiving is ripe for the comedy picking!

I'm not suggesting you go out and try stand-up, although that would take your mind off of caregiving, I can assure you! I am suggesting that you laugh when it's funny. Laugh in retrospect, and share those hilarious moments with the appropriate people, or Jimmy Kimmel or anyone else you think could use it.

Make it a habit to watch funny movies, television shows, read the comics. Do all this with your caregivee if possible. Both of you laughing together is a medicine no doctor will prescribe, but I know for a fact it makes both of your days better.

I am hoping to get back to Story Slams which you will find on my YouTube Channel where almost all my tales are about caregiving! These events are five-minute stories about a topic that I have always twisted to the caregiving tale with a humorous bent because, well once a caregiver for eight different people, you got stories, people!

If you are a caregiver or you are looking at it in the face right now, or if you have been and your journey has ended, I thank you for your service. It's hard, it's frustrating, and it's hilarious. Best of luck to you and feel free to email me at cathy.sikorski@gmail.com if you care to discuss!

Hopefully, the conversation samples in the book will help you get started with the difficult chats that you must do now, the looming need for preparation for your elders or yourself, or just a way to approach some things you hadn't thought about until this moment when you are thinking about it!

Thanks for joining me in important work to talk about caregiving. Go forth and have those critical conversations, and don't forget to take your sense of humor with you to the meeting. It does wonders for the atmosphere!

And for those of you who aren't sure if you are a caregiver or not, here are a few tips:

"You might be a Caregiver..."

1. If you know Medicare's phone number and website without Googling...You might be a Caregiver...

2. If your search for an Assisted Living Community for your mom starts to look like a nice vacation spot for you and your spouse...You might be a Caregiver

3. If you cancel your dentist appointment to attend Ice Cream Social Wednesday at your dad's nursing home, because you want the ice cream...You might be a Caregiver

4. If you know your parents' Medicare number, AARP number, United Healthcare number but not your own cell phone number...You might be a Caregiver

5. If you feel the need to correct WebMD about all the missed additional symptoms of a urinary tract infection...You might be a Caregiver

6. If your iPhone calendar has words on it like "catheters," "hearing aid," "urologist," or "dentures"...You might be a Caregiver

7. If going to the Emergency Room is like Cheers where they know your first name and how you take your coffee...You might be a Caregiver

8. If you took the black Sharpie to your husband's underwear to mark it for the wash instead of your mom's for the nursing home...You might be a Caregiver

9. If you've had more knock-down, drag-out fights with Insurance Companies, Hospitals and Doctor's office than Muhammad Ali...You might be a Caregiver

10. If everyone around you thinks you are speaking in tongues because you are constantly saying, PT, OT, UTI, or DME...You might be a Caregiver

SOMETIMES YOU JUST HAVE TO SLEEP ON IT!

MARGOT: Mom, Dad, I made an appointment with an Elder Lawyer to get some paperwork in order.

MOM: Margot, why would you need an Elder Lawyer, you're like 25!

MARGOT: Mom, I'm 30 and thanks for the compliment, but it's an appointment for you guys, not me.

DAD: We don't need an Elder Lawyer. We're not elder. We're not even old.

MARGOT: Dad.

DAD: Margot.

MARGOT: Dad, this is not about being old. This is about being prepared and planning.

MOM: Oh, we have plans.

MARGOT: You do?

MOM: Sure. We're going to move in with you!

DAD: No, we're not. At least I'm not. I'm dying.

MARGOT AND MOM: DAD!!!

DAD: What? I'm not moving in with anyone. I like my stuff where it is.

MARGOT: Well, first of all. Thanks, I guess. And second, Dad...and Mom, for that matter, see what I mean? You have two different ideas. You need to discuss this, because obviously, you haven't.

DAD: Nothing to discuss.

MOM: Nope. Nothing.

MARGOT: Fine. Well, if something happens to either of you. Who is going to help you?

MOM: Well, you and your sister, of course.

MARGOT: And how are we going to do that? Our names aren't on any of your accounts. We have no access to your banks, your doctors, anything. How are we going to do that?

DAD: Whoa! Wait a minute! You kids don't need to be in our affairs!

MARGOT: Dad, Mom, the last thing we want is to 'be in your affairs.' Trust me.

DAD: Good, then that's settled.

MOM: Good, let's have lunch.

MARGOT: GUYS! Sorry, that was a little loud. It's not settled. Unless you're going to the lawyer.

MOM: Oh, that seems excessive, dear.

DAD: Yes, what your mother said.

MARGOT: Okay, fine. I just want you to know that my sister and I love you very much. When the court decides to take all your money and put some stranger in charge of your whereabouts, we will be sure and come visit you. If they will let us.

MOM: Oh, don't be so dramatic dear.

MARGOT: Nope. You're right. This is all about you and your decisions. I'm sure your financial guy gave you good advice and you have nothing to worry about. I'm sure he told you about Powers of Attorney and the new Secure Act and the cost of home care or a nursing home should you need it. I'm sure he told you NOT to let your children know anything about your affairs, or be in charge in a crisis or emergency. I'm sure you have new wills where Rachel and I aren't toddlers who need a guardian and your grandchildren are protected. No worries. Yes, let's have lunch.

DAD: Fine. Lunch.

MOM: Yes, I made your favorite.

Later, much later. Like days, weeks even....MARGOT remains silent on this issue.

MOM: George.

DAD: What, Martha? It's bedtime.

MOM: You know she was right, don't you?

DAD: Who?

MOM: Don't pretend, George.

DAD: Okay, fine. Call Margot and tell her to make the appointment.

Sometimes, you just gotta' let it go. Let your loved ones come to the place or not. You can lead a horse to water............

ACKNOWLEDGEMENTS

No woman is an island. I have had countless people support me in my mission to help caregivers plan and prepare so that they can have the best life as they try to create the best life for the people they care for. Many have gotten on board to look at legal issues and financial issues in a new a different way. And for that I am eternally grateful.

A special thanks to my Beta readers, Jean Dames, Terri Newmyer, and my cousin, a wonderful writer in her own right, Sue Repko. Their advice and suggestions were invaluable in making this a clearer and more enjoyable read. That's saying a lot, since no one wants to talk about this topic! Thanks to my Publisher Extraordinaire, Donna Cavanagh and her right-hand man, Ed Cavanagh of HOPress and Corner Office Books for their full support as the publisher of this, my third book, and all my books. They are kind, wise, extraordinarily helpful in publishing, marketing and promotion. Lucky for me, they are now my very dear friends.

Every time I write a book, I am convinced it is my last one. I want to name every friend I ever had, every person I ever met who would discuss caregiving with me, and every colleague on Facebook, LinkedIn, and Twitter who is steeped in the mission to help our caregivers at each stage of their lives. I can say that because I have been blessed with years and years to make friends and collect colleagues the list would be as long as this book! And I really hate it when I forget to put in someone's name. It's so embarrassing! So, for all you friends and colleagues who are too numerous to mention after an infinite number of conversations and badgering by me, asking me questions, and even sometimes taking my advice, I say to each and every one of you, thank you, thank you, thank you. You make me think this work is important even if you are just humoring me...I hope I'm humoring you, too!

About the Author:

Cathy Sikorski is a consulting and practicing attorney for over 30 years and limits her practice to Elder Law issues. She has been a significant caregiver for eight different family members and friends. This combination of legal and practical experience in aging and caregiving has made her a sought-out speaker on these important issues.

Sikorski is a frequent guest on television, radio programs, podcasts and also speaks regularly at conferences where she educates audiences on financial and legal preparation for the aging crisis.

With more than 30 years of law behind her, she provides critical legal information for our aging population and those who serve them. *12 Conversations* is Sikorski's third book. Her first two books include a humorous memoir *Showering with Nana: Confessions of a Serial (killer) Caregiver (HumorOutcasts Press 2015)* and *Who Moved My Teeth? Preparing for Self, Loved Ones and Caregiving* which debuted at #1 on Amazon *(Corner Office Books 2016)*.

Sikorski has appeared as Keynote Speaker at many events including the National Caregivers Conferences in Chicago and Philadelphia. She has participated in memoir writing classes for two years at the prestigious Fine Arts Work Center in Provincetown, Massachusetts and her work won a Humor Award at Philadelphia Writer's Conference. Her One-Act Play, *All Caregiving Aside,* was performed by the Writers Theatre of New Jersey at Kean University during the Healing VoicesOnStage: Caregivers' Stories.

Sikorski has been featured on the Huffington Post, AARP and is a SheSource expert for the Women's Media Center (WMC) in Washington, D.C. She serves on the Board of Directors of Nancy's House, a nonprofit dedicated to respite care for caregivers. Sikorski is a contributing author for the HumorOutcasts.com website, and she can be seen on the West Chester Story Slam YouTube channel. Readers can catch up on her work and her speaking schedule by visiting her blog *You just have to Laugh...where Caregiving is Comedy...*at www.cathysikorski.com and www.cathysikorski.com/Speaker